About the Author

Judith A. Schickedanz is Professor of Education at Boston University. She has been a preschool teacher and has worked closely with practicing preschool teachers throughout her career. Currently, she is a member of the Early Literacy Committee within the International Reading Association and is coeditor of the *Asia-Pacific Journal of Research in Early Childhood Education*. Among her publications are *Writing in Preschool*, with Renée M. Casbergue (International Reading Association, 2004); *Much More Than the ABCs* (NAEYC, 1999); and *Curriculum in Early Childhood* (Allyn & Bacon, 1997). She received her doctorate in early childhood education from the University of Illinois.

Acknowledgements

The writing of a book has always brought to mind specific people as well as the debts of gratitude I owe them. This book is no exception. *Increasing the Power of Instruction* has been influenced and inspired by my former teachers, close colleagues, numerous authors and researchers, doctoral students, and of course, children.

Over the past 25 years, my involvement with people in the following programs has been especially important: the Boston University Preschool (1984–2001); the Chelsea, MA–Boston University Collaborative (1990–93); the Appletree Institute Charter School in Washington, DC (2001–05); and the Springfield, MA, Early Education Collaborative, Early Reading First Project (2003–07). With this involvement, I had a front-row seat in many classrooms and access to the wise counsel and support of many dedicated people interested in exploring new paths of instruction for preschool children. I am especially grateful to Mary Lynn Pergantis, Bethany Sanders Leahy, Jan Kanosky Nagler, and Annmarie Blaney, lead teachers in the Boston University Laboratory School; Molly Collins, Wen-Feng Lai, Young-mi Lee, and Elida Laski, doctoral students at BU; Dr. Joan Ottinger, who served as the Early Childhood Director for the Chelsea-BU Collaborative; and Susan Gosselin, Michelle Keating, and Mary Horn, all coaches in the Springfield Early Reading First Project.

This book has benefited enormously from the attention it received from the editorial staff at NAEYC. In particular, Carol Copple offered encouragement and direction throughout the entire process of developing the book. It is no exaggeration to say that a finished book would not have materialized without her support. And Natalie Klein Cavanagh worked wonders as she transformed clumsy drafts into a streamlined and coherent manuscript. For this help, especially at critical moments, I shall always be grateful.

Increasing the Power of Instruction

Integration of Language, Literacy, and Math Across the Preschool Day

Judith A. Schickedanz

National Association for the Education of Young Children
Washington, DC

National Association for
the Education of
Young Children
1313 L Street NW, Suite 500
Washington, DC 20005-4101
202-232-8777 • 800-424-2460
www.naeyc.org

NAEYC Books
Director, Publications and
Educational Initiatives
Carol Copple

Managing Editor
Bry Pollack

Design and Production
Malini Dominey

Editorial Associate
Cassandra Berman

Editorial Assistant
Melissa Edwards

Permissions
Lacy Thompson

Marketing Director
Matt Munroe

Through its publications
program, the National
Association for the Education
of Young Children (NAEYC)
provides a forum for
discussion of major issues
and ideas in the early
childhood field, with the
hope of provoking thought
and promoting professional
growth. The views expressed
or implied in this book are
not necessarily those of the
Association or its members.

Permissions

Illustration from *Inch by Inch* (New York: Astor-Honor), copyright © 1960 by Leo Lionni, renewed 1988 by Leo Lionni. Reprinted by permission of Ann Lionni and Astor-Honor, Inc.

Illustrations from *Ten Black Dots* (Greenwillow Books), copyright © 1986 by Donald Crews. Reprinted by permission of HarperCollins Publishers.

Credits

Front cover photographs (*clockwise from top*)—Copyright © by Sharon LeVine; Susan Schaden; Rich Graessle; and Ellen B. Senisi. *Author photo*—Copyright © by Boston University.

Illustrations by Natalie Klein Cavanagh, copyright © NAEYC.

Increasing the Power of Instruction: Integration of Language, Literacy, and Math Across the Preschool Day

Developmental editing: Natalie Klein Cavanagh.

Library of Congress Control Number: 2008920740
ISBN: 978-1-928896-51-7
NAEYC Item #239

Contents

Introduction

Four-year-old Jason pages through a book about lizards in his preschool's library corner, then calls out to his teacher, Ms. Freeman.

Jason: Hey! This green lizard looks like the one in our raccoon book. What is it?

Ms. Freeman: Well, let's take a look at the book to find the lizard's name. Oh, it says that this is a *green anole* lizard. It also says that this big, red part sticking out from under the lizard's throat is called a *dewlap*.

Jason: A what?

Ms. Freeman: A dewlap. Can you say that word?

Jason: Dewlap.

Ms. Freeman: And you are right—it is the same kind of lizard as the one pictured in the story about the little raccoon that we read today!

Jason: It's right here. [He turns to a specific page in his book.]

Ms. Freeman: Oh, yes. I see it. I wonder. . . .

At just this moment, Ms. Freeman is interrupted by a child's call from the easel in the art center.

Maria: My s doesn't look right. I need some help!

Ms. Freeman excuses herself from the library corner, promising to return in a few minutes, if she can.

A day in an early childhood classroom can be hectic. There is so much that we could choose to do, so many skills and concepts on which to work. How can a teacher do it all? Over the past few years, I have heard many preschool teachers' concerns that teaching and learning have become too fragmented by subject curriculum areas and devoid of meaningful context. There are hardly enough hours in a day to teach everything we are asked to teach. This is especially true when the instruction for one time period addresses only one content domain.

If done well, however, **increasing the integration of learning within multiple content domains and various instructional contexts can help us better manage our time and make our instruction more powerful—and learning more meaningful—for children.**

Toward that goal, this book focuses on *how* teachers can increase the power of their instruction, providing examples and descriptions of ways that integration can deepen preschool children's learning, specifically in language, literacy, and mathematics. Although other content domains do come into play in the examples provided throughout, this book discusses those three domains because today's preschool teachers are grappling with demands to provide more instruction in those important areas.

Current literature

Some resources available to teachers already describe ways to support preschool children's language, literacy, and math learning simultaneously and in a wide variety of contexts. For example, *Teaching Our Youngest*, a short booklet published by the U.S. Department of Education and the U.S. Department of Health and Human Services, Early Childhood–Head Start Task Force (2002), suggests ways to embed language, literacy, and math instruction in daily routines.

Similarly, numerous books on early literacy learning (including Neuman, Copple, & Bredekamp 2000; Heroman & Jones 2004; Bennett-Armistead, Duke, & Moses 2005; Vukelich, Christie, & Enz 2008) provide examples of children's use of print in play contexts and give suggestions for using field trips and play with concrete materials to enhance children's oral vocabulary and literacy skills. (For example, before visiting a local supermarket, the teacher reads a book to the children about supermarkets. After the field trip, as the children set up a play store, the teacher helps them make labels for the shelves and a sign indicating the store's hours.) Books focusing on the project approach (e.g., Helm & Katz 2001; Helm & Beneke 2003), in which an investigation is pursued in depth across a variety of contexts, also demonstrate how learning can encompass multiple subject domains.

Several chapters in *Mathematics in the Early Years* (1999), edited by Juanita Copley, focus on learning mathematics in a variety of ways: in conjunction with puzzles, Lego pieces, and blocks (Ginsburg, Inoue, & Seo 1999); within the context of musical experiences (Kim 1999); and through opportunities provided by the outdoor environment (Basile 1999). Several researchers have investigated the use of books and storytelling to teach early childhood mathematics (see, e.g., Casey, Kersh, & Young 2004; Schiro 2004). For example, Haekyung Hong's discussion of using storybooks to teach mathematics (in Copley 1999) suggests choosing stories that have mathematical problems that are integral to the plot. She also suggests making materials available that are related to the story, such as hats when reading Esphyr Slobodkina's *Caps for Sale*. Children can use such materials to reenact the math problems in the books, which fosters greater comprehension. For example, the children's familiarity with *Caps for Sale* might interest them in counting and grouping the hats that the teacher provided. Hong says that this may increase children's motivation to engage in math activities during choice time. Hong also hints at ways that story discussions or retellings might be used for highlighting mathematical vocabulary or concepts, and she notes the importance of ensuring that in any interactions about math or other subjects, teachers take care not to interfere with children's story enjoyment and comprehension.

Hong's suggestions are more selective and nuanced than those found in many other resources (e.g., Griffiths & Clyne 1991; Schiro 1997; Evans, Leija, & Falkner 2001). These resources often identify a wide array of picture books that are suitable for embedding mathematics instruction, and they provide suggestions for doing so. For example, in a story about a growing child, they may suggest discussing size differences and measurement. In a story in which there is a considerable passage of time, they may highlight possibilities for teaching the days of the week or the structure of a calendar. If many items appear in an illustration, teachers are encouraged to ask children to count them. While such strategies may have their place in providing mathematics instruction, they do not truly integrate the math and literacy domains, as the literacy content is not suitably explored along with the math.

Although all these resources are helpful to teachers, there is a need for more information and for material of a somewhat different kind. Specifically, teachers need resources that illustrate and model *how* to integrate learning, especially in the critical areas of oral language, literacy, and mathematics, while at the same time making sure that instruction is robust.

The power of true integration

The overall purpose for integrating curriculum is to increase the learning in *all* integrated domains. With this in mind, the book adheres to several guidelines for the integration of learning. Specifically, teachers should:

1. Ensure that taking action to support learning in one domain does not undermine learning in another domain.

2. Consider timing when integrating. If an opportunity arises in the midst of an activity, ask yourself if a potential detour is likely to add enough to make the "trip" worthwhile, especially if there's an opportunity later to integrate.

3. Take into consideration children's learning sequences and their present knowledge in each domain.

4. Think carefully about the emphasis to be given to each domain, depending on the learning goals and instructional context.

5. Consider integrating not only within one instructional experience, but also across multiple and related instructional experiences.

6. Think strategically about using multiple instructional contexts, such as whole group, small group, or center time. Ask yourself, "What is the most appropriate and effective context for each part of the learning I wish to integrate?"

These guidelines are applicable to integration in general, and can be used with other content domains outside the focus of this book, such as science or the arts.

Integration across content domains

One way to integrate curriculum is to mesh together two or more content domains within one instructional activity and context, where a teacher might previously have focused on just one content domain. For example, mathematical concepts might be explored during story time, extending the focus beyond the main plot of the story or the thoughts and feelings of the characters. Similarly, some writing and use of print and an emphasis on oral language might be incorporated into a small group math activity, broadening the focus beyond math concepts such as number or measurement. The teacher might chart the results of children's findings, such as the number of cubes versus the number of Popsicle sticks required to measure the length of a table, and then help the children to create written headings for the chart. Or, a teacher might incorporate short verbal math problems into a board game, where the answer to the math problem could determine the number of places a child moves his or her marker on the board.

Integration across settings

In another kind of integration, opportunities for children's learning within a given domain—or in multiple domains—are supported throughout the day in a variety of settings. For example, a book's full potential to support math learning might be realized in a small group session, rather than when it is read to children for the first time. Similarly, rather than schedule all math explorations of one kind for a single small group setting, a teacher might instead use small groups first to introduce a set of materials and support children's initial understanding of a particular math concept, and then to introduce additional materials for independent use during center time, allowing children to extend their exploration of the concept into a different context.

In the opening vignette, for example, Ms. Freeman set the stage for literacy learning to occur in different contexts. After the children listened to a book that included a lizard as a character, she made information books about lizards and related animals available in the library for children's use during center time. These books could further their knowledge of themes introduced in the story children were read earlier.

Learning contexts in the preschool day

Because we will be discussing instruction in several different settings, it is worthwhile to define just what we mean by each of these arrangements and groupings. The daily schedule in a preschool revolves around a variety of *learning contexts*. These contexts vary in the number of children involved, in the kinds of learning activities they can accommodate, in their duration, and in the roles adopted by the children and the teacher. The major features of the three learning contexts highlighted in this book are noted in the table on the following page and discussed below.

Whole group

All children in the class participate together in *whole group* learning contexts. In many preschool classrooms, the daily circle time and the daily story time are whole group activities. The teacher typically leads and plans whole group activities and has a variety of specific learning goals in mind. In a whole group activity, children are expected to listen (to a book, an explanation, or directions) and respond. The activity at hand determines the kind of response—ranging from spontaneous comments, as when a child expresses excitement about an event in a story, to answering a specific question posed by the teacher, to offering ideas for solving a problem, to joining in with the rest of the children in singing a song or reciting a poem. Children may use their hands and bodies to perform movements that accompany these songs and poems.

In a whole group, children might also watch the teacher's demonstrations, listen to and comment on the teacher's explanations, look at pictures in books as the teacher reads, follow along as the teacher runs a finger under the text on a poster or book cover, and follow the plot of an unfolding story. Children use their language and math skills as they generate words that rhyme or consider a verbal math problem the teacher poses. For the most part, whole group learning contexts do not involve activities in which children physically manipulate and explore concrete materials.

Because whole group contexts typically require children to sit on the floor, attend to the teacher, and engage in a variety of cognitively stimulating activities with little or no physical activity, these activities are kept relatively short. For example, a daily story time might be allotted 15 to 20 minutes; daily circle time, perhaps 20 to 25 minutes. These two whole group learning contexts do not take place back to back. Intervening activities of different

kinds occur, and these allow for exploration, conversation, and physical movement. Balancing a schedule in this way helps avoid situations in which preschoolers are asked to sit too long. No matter how varied and engaging the whole group learning context, preschoolers' attention and cognitive resources wane if they are required to sit too long and engage in a single activity.

Small group

Small group learning contexts accommodate a portion of the class—sometimes only two or three children, sometimes as many as ten. Teachers typically plan activities for small groups that meet specific learning goals in a particular content domain, such as literacy, math, or science. Sometimes a teacher introduces a new concept or skill; at other times a teacher follows up previously introduced concepts or skills with activities that provide additional practice and exposure. A small group activity typically lasts from 25 to 30 minutes, often with the teacher guiding much of the children's participation. Typically several groups of children are engaged simultaneously in several different activities. According to the activity, one of these groups might receive close guidance and support from one teacher. The other two groups are given activities that can be done more independently; a second teacher can facilitate both of these.

Many small group activities involve the physical manipulation of materials. For example, children might test different kinds of materials to see if they absorb or repel water; use a variety of geometric shapes to make a tangram picture; or use markers to draw pictures, and then discuss them with one another and the teacher.

Other small group activities do not involve manipulation of materials. For example, children might be asked to indicate their favorite flavor of ice cream from among three or four choices, and then watch as the teacher records their votes in the form of a graph. No matter the specific activity, the benefit of a small group learning context is that a teacher can observe each child's understanding

Features of three different preschool learning contexts

Whole Group
All of the children in the class participate together—typically 15 to 20 children.

Activities, Content, and Participation:
Teacher determines activities and their content.
Child participation is not a choice. Children are expected to join the group.

Examples:
Story Time
15 to 20 minutes*

Circle Time
20 to 25 minutes*

Roles:
Teacher leads.
Children listen to the story and participate in discussion. Comment and ask questions. Help the teacher read the title; chime in on familiar portions of the text.

Teacher leads.
Children listen, sing songs, recite poems, engage in finger/hand and body motions, answer questions, engage in literacy and math tasks, and participate in discussion.

Small Group
Part of the class participate in the activity together, with group size ranging between two and ten.

Activities, Content, and Participation:
Teacher determines activities and their content, and composes the small groups.
Child participation typically is not a choice. Many activities allow and encourage children to use their own ideas and to express their own thoughts.

Examples:
Science Activities
Math Activities
Literacy Activities

Roles:
Teacher leads and guides, interacts with individuals, and responds to individual questions and comments.

Children manipulate materials, answer questions, offer ideas, experiment, solve problems collaboratively, and help to record what they observe.

Duration:
25 to 30 minutes*

Center Time
Children engage in activities as individuals, with a peer partner, and in small groups of two to seven children.

Activities, Content, and Participation:
Teacher determines array of materials and activity choices, but takes children's interests into consideration when making these decisions.
Children choose where they will work and play, and have considerable latitude in directing the use of materials to suit their interests and ideas. Children enter and leave activities as they wish (within certain boundaries, such as the number of children that a particular activity will accommodate).

Examples:
Water and Sand Area
Art Table and Easel
Puzzles, Literacy Manipulatives, Math Manipulatives Area
Book Area
Writing Area
Nature/Science Area
Block Area
Dramatic Play Area

Roles:
Teacher supports, assists, and provides help and instruction when needed. Teacher converses with children as they pursue their chosen activities.
Children actively engage with materials, interact with other children, and initiate and direct much of their activity. Children engage with teachers to receive help, support, information, and to involve them in role play.

Duration:
55 to 60 minutes*

*The shorter time is appropriate for half-day programs.

and approach more readily, provide more specific directions for the children who need them, and tailor feedback to a child's specific needs.

Sometimes, the small group activity is scheduled during center time (discussed in more detail below). In this approach, one teacher leads the small group activity while the other teacher (or teachers) provides support for all of the centers, and children rotate between small groups and centers. While this is a common practice, conducting a small group activity in conjunction with center time presents various problems (which is why in this book we largely discuss the two separately). First, the children in the small group are sometimes distracted by the center time activities of other children. Although center time should never be loud and wild, it will, at times, be appropriately boisterous, as children engage in play. A second problem arises in providing the level of interaction and support that the remaining fourteen or fifteen children need as they engage in center time activities. This can be quite a challenge for one teacher. Because of this, teachers may feel the need to reduce the number of center time activities, which may in turn limit learning opportunities. This situation diminishes the enrichment that center time should provide.

Children also participate in small groups during snack times and mealtimes. Although each child eats his or her own food, children often sit in small groups at tables that can accommodate only five or six children. The teacher can form the membership of the group for each table for the duration of a month or so, then the groups can be reformed periodically to encourage children to get acquainted with more classmates and to reduce or increase the social challenges in a specific group. To the extent possible, teachers eat and talk with the children, supporting social interaction and language and concept development. Because mealtimes and snack times provide unique learning opportunities—both social and otherwise—they are important small group times.

Center time

Center time, which is sometimes also referred to as *choice time*, allows for a variety of groupings of children, from a single child, to pairs of children, to small groups of three to six or seven children. During center time, the children group themselves by choosing where and with whom they wish to work and play. The physical environment (e.g., the floor space in the block area, the number of chairs at a table) and the kinds of materials available (e.g., the number of easels in the classroom) also help determine the size of the groupings and the extent of flow in and out of an area or activity.

Many materials provided for use during center time are open-ended, which allows children to create their own play scenarios. For example, even though vehicles of various kinds might be available in the block area (perhaps prompting dramatic play with pretend highways or construction sites), the children might instead build houses with the blocks and bring over dolls from the playhouse. Similarly, although the dramatic play area might be stocked with props for feeding, bathing, and putting babies to bed, children might prefer to haul their babies and food supplies from the kitchen to the library corner, where they will spread out blankets and have a picnic. The children might select a space because it is the only open area available in the room. Then they transform it mentally—they pretend they are outside having a picnic, ignoring the tubs or shelves of books surrounding them. Pretend play allows for such transformation of reality. A preschool teacher expects children to use materials during center time to support their own ideas, and she values children's demonstrations of initiative and creativity. Outdoor time (which is beyond the scope of this book) and center time are particularly useful in encouraging these activities for children.

Children will also gather into small groups of their own choosing for various center time activities. For example, a group of four to six children might sit together at the art table to make a collage or to finger-paint, and groups of four or five children often collaborate to build structures in the block area. During center time, children move in and out of these groupings as they wish and as space allows, with teachers also moving around the room as needed. Here and there, a teacher provides very direct and explicit instruction, and may engage with a single child for several minutes. For example, a child might call out for help while writing her name on a painting at the easel, or when she is experiencing a problem assembling a jigsaw puzzle.

Center time, however, is usually not the most effective context for an activity planned by the teacher to teach a new concept or skill, because such activities cannot be given the level of sustained support and guidance typically required. A teacher-led group setting is the usual context for introducing new ideas; afterwards some materials and activities can appropriately be placed in an area for children's more independent use during center time.

Given the range of options available during center time and the opportunities for children to take initiative and create, center time is allocated a longer period of time in the preschool day than any other learning context. The specific amount of time depends on the length of the preschool's day, with half-day programs offering a shorter center time than longer programs.

Approach

We know that language, literacy, and math skills, as well as other content knowledge acquired during the early years, vary widely across different groups of children, and that they are strong predictors of children's later success in school (Juel 1988; Storch & Whitehurst 2002; NICHD Early Child Care Research Network 2005; Hoff 2006; Duncan et al. 2007; Ginsburg, Lee, & Boyd 2008). Research indicates that effective preschool programming emphasizes these areas and provides the full range of learning contexts and instructional strategies needed to support different aspects of learning and development (Bowman, Donavan, & Burns 2001).

Seeking to cover all curriculum subject areas, some early childhood programs today have greatly reduced time for play and independent engagement with materials. Given their unique contributions to children's learning, reducing opportunities for play and independent engagement with materials during center time is a mistake. In other preschool classrooms, whole and small group instructional segments are not yet part of the daily schedule. Instruction in these group contexts can be developmentally appropriate and should be added where it is missing to provide the range of opportunities that are known to support children's learning (see, e.g., Justice et al. 2003). This book also provides guidance and models for best practice while working in such groups.

Some readers may question the amount of space this book allocates to teacher-led group instruction compared with the amount of space it allocates to choice time. This is not meant to suggest that choice time is of less value. A balance between choice time and teacher-guided group experiences best supports children's learning (Senechal & LeFevre 2002; Justice et al. 2003; Dickinson & Porche 2005). Using a variety of groupings and settings also increases the likelihood that *all* children in the class will have access to the teacher's scaffolding and instruction (Layzer, Goodson, & Moss 1993; Dickinson, McCabe, & Essex 2006).

As a whole, this book focuses on increasing the power of instruction in the domains of mathematics, oral language, and literacy. Powerful instruction, by definition, must be interesting, meaningful, and engaging, for if children's attention and engagement are diminished, so too is their learning (Torgesen et al. 2001; Justice et al. 2003; Dickinson & Porche 2005; Spira, Bracken, & Fischell 2005; Duncan et al. 2007). This book provides vivid portraits of classroom practice, most of which are based on my observation of teachers over the course of many years and in a variety of contexts.

The examples in this book incorporate teachers' advice and experience in integrated classroom situations. They do not focus on classroom management or on explaining rules. Nor do they focus on a teacher merely leading children in counting or naming letters. Rather, the examples focus on interactions that extend children's knowledge and draw their attention to important differences in patterns, such as those in print and speech. They also model strategies that increase children's understanding of a concept, rather than focus only on supporting children in mastering a skill. These situations feature teaching that is intentional, explicit, and preplanned; the instruction featured is not, however, formal, as it is in curriculum that provides a complete set of prescribed lessons, allowing little—if any—room for a teacher's judgment in selection and adaptation (Schickedanz 2003; Epstein 2007).

The structure of this book mirrors the two different ways that teachers can achieve this through the integration of instruction. Part I is subject-focused and deals with integration across content domains; Part II considers integration across learning contexts. This organization reinforces the twofold nature of integration, demonstrating how teachers can maximize instruction and make the most of the preschool day.

The examples of teaching in this book cover two whole group contexts (story time and circle time), as well as small groups and center time. Many of the book's examples are portraits of instruction provided by a hypothetical teacher who is both effective and experienced. These examples are inspired by the many teachers I have been fortunate enough to work with over the years.

At the end of Chapters 2 through 7, you will also find questions to help you reflect on the teaching examples and integration principles introduced. Consider your own teaching experience or knowledge of children's learning styles as you think about and discuss these questions.

This book is not a curriculum guide. Such a guide would address all of the learning standards in mathematics, oral language, and literacy; and it would provide guidance for creating coherent and comprehensive experiences in ways that build knowledge systematically over time. This book does not attempt to address all of the skills that should be included in a preschool curriculum. Moreover, it does not include an organized, year-long plan for instruction in language, literacy, or mathematics. What *is* offered in this volume is information and examples that I hope will inspire and model integration of learning as an approach to creating more powerful instruction. I also hope to inspire a balance in instruction—giving more attention to math and ensuring that we provide the rich language required for long-term success in literacy, rather than focusing literacy instruction too narrowly on print skills.

I Integration Across Content Domains

1

Integrating Learning Across the Domains Through Story Reading

A major focus of this book is the integration of learning in the context of reading aloud to children. In particular, these next chapters look at integration across the domains of language, literacy, and mathematics through reading books aloud—first with storybooks and later with "predictable" books.

Many resources on integrating mathematics instruction with story reading lack detailed guidance about balancing instruction among math, literacy, and language. Instead, they often focus narrowly on embedding mathematics instruction into stories or on using a story as a jumping-off point to introduce a related math activity. They neglect to consider carefully whether the instruction is suitable for the specific story or is presented in a way that also supports oral language, story comprehension, and literacy skills. As a result, these resources do not provide guidance that truly supports integration as defined in this book. Embedding mathematics instruction that way may not only undermine and diminish children's language and literacy learning but also lessen the extent to which the story increases mathematics learning, putting all learning at risk.

To illustrate what can happen when a storybook is read for the sole purpose of introducing a math activity, without also considering goals for language

and literacy, consider the ineffective use of Leo Lionni's storybook *Inch by Inch*, described below.

In *Inch by Inch*, an inchworm escapes becoming a hungry robin's dinner by demonstrating his usefulness in measuring things. The robin invites the inchworm to measure his tail; then, impressed by the inchworm's skill and knowledge, the robin flies the inchworm to other birds to measure various parts of their bodies, too. Near the end of the story, a nightingale threatens to eat the inchworm unless he can measure her song. The inchworm offers to try, but inches away to safety while the nightingale sings, absorbed in her song and oblivious to his escape. So what might a well-intentioned but ineffective effort at integration look like?

> The teacher does not make comments during the reading of this story and afterward does not engage the children in any discussion of the story's theme, characters, or plot. Instead, immediately after reading the story, the teacher tells the children that they will be doing some measuring, "just as the inchworm did." The teacher then explains basic measuring and gives directions for an activity in which children measure with both standard and nonstandard units, using rulers and Popsicle sticks.

Following up a story with a related math activity, like this teacher did, is a good idea. Instructional power is increased, however, if a story is also used to support language and literacy, and if a math concept that is central to the story's plot is introduced to the children and explored within the context of the story as an integral part of supporting children's overall comprehension of the narrative. This is what the teacher did *not* do. Children's comprehension of the narrative can suffer if the math activity is emphasized without also ensuring that the children truly understand the story on which it is based.

The next chapters explore in more depth a fuller use of the same storybook, with examples of teachers supporting learning in mathematics as well as language and literacy. But before delving more extensively into teaching examples of integration, we should consider preschool children's comprehension of narrative and language development. Understanding the challenges that young children face in these areas, and the strategies that are effective in helping children meet these challenges, helps teachers adequately plan to support all aspects of children's learning through story reading.

Story comprehension

Stories are narratives, with a typical structure that is sometimes referred to as a *story grammar* (Stein 1988; Benson 1993). As such, stories have specific features that are presented somewhat predictably. For example, they have characters, a setting, and a plot and typically involve a problem that characters try to solve. The story's plot is the sequence of events, usually leading to the solution of the problem. In stories, characters' actions are fueled by motives and goals that are informed by what characters know, understand, and feel. Narratives can be nonfiction, but those read in the early childhood classroom are generally fiction (as are the narratives discussed in the next two chapters).

Preschoolers face many challenges as they try to understand stories. To understand a character's actions in a story, or the story's setting(s) and events, the reader or listener draws upon his or her own prior knowledge and the information the text provides. As the story proceeds, the reader or listener actively thinks and reasons to comprehend the story. Cognitive skills are needed to understand the relationship between a character's thoughts and actions, and to fill in information that is not explicitly stated in the text or depicted in the illustrations. It takes considerable experience with books in supportive contexts for preschoolers to learn how to think about and understand narratives, and for them to gain the background knowledge required to understand many stories fully. Preschoolers have relatively little background knowledge; their reasoning skills are also somewhat limited. Moreover, these two characteristics of young children interact—a lack of knowledge about something limits a preschooler's ability to think logically about it (Brown 1989). It is no wonder, then, that preschoolers need support in understanding the stories we read aloud to them.

Teacher strategies

Considerable research-based information exists about how to effectively support young children's understanding of stories (e.g., Beck & McKeown 2001; McGee & Schickedanz 2007). For example, we know that children's understanding of a story the first time it is read to them can be supported by a teacher's comments and questions during reading. We also know that asking questions that encourage reflection after the story is finished further increases children's understanding.

Sometimes, teachers of children in kindergarten and primary school are advised to provide support through the use of thoughtful questions as they read children a particular story for the first time (Beck & McKeown 2001). Problems can arise, however, when *preschool* teachers rely too heavily on questions and give too few explanations. Given preschoolers' limited background knowledge and reasoning skills, their responses to higher-level questions often miss the mark. Although a child's response sometimes is related to the question posed by the teacher, its relationship to the text is often no more than tangential (Neuman 1999; Beck & McKeown 2001). When this happens, many preschool teachers feel uncomfortable correcting children's responses, as they do not want to discourage participation.

Guiding a preschooler toward a better understanding of a story is not a simple matter, and it often requires a rather lengthy individual conversation. As a conversation is pursued with the one child, the other children may become frustrated and then disengage. This is especially true if a teacher stops frequently during the first reading of a story to pose questions that lead to several lengthy conversations with a couple of children. Surveying all the children during the first reading of a story also creates long breaks in the narrative, during which it is sometimes difficult to maintain the interest and engagement of all children in the group. It can also be difficult for children to follow the plot and theme of a story if there are too many breaks in a reading. (For an example of a story reading that gets off-topic, see Box 1.1.)

To avoid this quagmire as they read to children, preschool teachers can think and wonder out loud, modeling the comprehension strategies that competent and experienced readers use (Cochran-Smith 1984; Duffy et al. 1987; Duffy & Roehler 1989; Smith 2006). These types of comments are

---

Box 1.1

Getting off-topic

The class is reading the book *One Dark Night*, by Hazel Hutchins, for the first time. The setting is a child's house and yard, at night, during a bad thunderstorm. A stray mother cat brings a kitten to the door, and Jonathan, the main character, lets her in. When the mother cat dashes back outside into the storm, Jonathan starts to follow her, but his grandfather pulls him back inside the house and closes the door. Let's look at how a question leads to an off-topic discussion at this point in the story:

Teacher: His grandfather doesn't want him to go outside right now. He pulled him back inside.

Jamie: Why?

Teacher: Who has an idea about why Jonathan's grandfather won't allow him to go outside?

Michelle: Because, because, because you can't go outside when it's dark.

Teacher: Uh-huh. Right. It's not a good idea. Let's get some other ideas.

Luis: Somebody out there could hurt him.

Teacher: Maybe. We would hope not, but maybe. Let's see what Keisha thinks.

Keisha: Well, because the little kitten is in the house, and he should stay with him.

Teacher: Oh, someone needs to take care of the little kitten the mother cat brought in. Yes, a good idea. Let's hear one more idea, and then we'll read more of the story and maybe we'll find out why Jonathan's grandfather didn't want him to go outside with the mother cat.

Sam: The cat could go down the street and then you could get runned over by a car at night.

Teacher: Oh, that would be terrible, wouldn't it? Sounds like there are a lot of reasons why Jonathan should stay in the house and not follow the cat outside. Okay, let's read some more of the story.

Although the children's responses included some good reasons why an adult would not want a child to go outside at night, none of the children mentioned the danger posed by a bad thunderstorm, which was probably among the grandfather's major concerns. Moreover, the children might get distracted from the story by all the other dangers they mentioned. The teacher sensed that the discussion was getting off-topic and the children were losing interest in the story, so she said, "Let's hear one more idea, and then we'll read more of the story…."

Instead, this teacher could easily have responded to Jamie's original question with a simple explanation, then returned to the story without a long and potentially distracting interruption. For example:

Teacher: Well, there's a bad storm outside—a thunderstorm with lightning and thunder. If you go outside during a thunderstorm, you'll get very wet and cold, plus lightning might hurt you. It's not safe. Jonathan's grandfather wanted him to be safe inside."

She then could have continued the story.

---

sometimes called *comprehension asides* (Schickedanz 2006; McGee & Schickedanz 2007). In this approach, children are not silent, nor are their minds passive. Rather, they think about and engage with the story and the teacher's comments. They can comment and ask questions, to which the teacher responds. While many of these responses should be limited to simple acknowledgments, a few must be more extensive—though still relatively short—to clarify a child's misunderstanding. In these instances, the teacher gives appropriate, concise explanations, considering both the needs of the individual child and the continued engagement of the other children in the group. The teacher avoids throwing most of the children's questions back to the group, for children's answers often go far afield, as in the example in Box 1.1 on the previous page.

When helpful comprehension asides are incorporated, children's own comments and questions are often more related to the story than they are when a teacher rarely shares his or her own knowledge and thinking. Comprehension asides are also quite helpful, even essential, when a teacher integrates math or other content domains into a story reading.

Even though a teacher's comments should primarily be explanatory during the first reading of a story, the teacher can still pose one or two thoughtful questions. Such questions prompt children's thinking about the story *after* they have a grasp of some relevant details, encouraging children to respond in ways that relate fairly directly to the text. Teachers may still need to provide some guidance as preschoolers answer these questions. Even so, because this approach supports thinking that is closer to the text, it helps the teacher avoid long interruptions.

Language development

Preschoolers are still learning the basics of oral language. Research is clear that the early years are a critical time for the development of a good oral vocabulary and competence in understanding *syntax*, or the rules for ordering words to create sentences (Hart & Risley 1995). Also both oral vocabulary and listening comprehension are intimately tied to reading achievement (Storch & Whitehurst 2002; Muter et al. 2004; NICHD Early Child Care Research Network 2005; Lonigan 2006; Senechal, Ouellette, & Rodney 2006). Oral vocabulary also affects beginning reading indirectly, through a relationship with *phonological awareness* (Lonigan 2006). In other words, there is a correlation between larger oral vocabularies and greater ease in learning to think of spoken words as an ordered series of individual sounds (*phonemes*) (Metsala & Walley 1998; Lonigan 2006).

It is also important to help young children develop a vocabulary related to math. Children should learn the meanings of words such as *more*, *less*, *bigger*, *smaller*, *a few*, *all*, *enough*, *measure*, and *count*. Learning these words not only supports children's learning in mathematics but also increases their understanding of stories, as this vocabulary appears frequently (especially when narratives have math content). A list of math-related vocabulary is provided in Table 1.1. (For more discussion of children's development of some key mathematical concepts, particularly *number, operations, geometry,* and *measurement*, see Appendix C.)

There is an important relationship between the richness of language children are exposed to and engage with and children's subsequent language development. For example, children gain vocabulary when they experience higher levels of adult talk (such as words less commonly used in everyday conversation) and higher levels of both semantic support (verbal explanations such as "A *ferocious* lion is one that is very, very mean and dangerous") and physical support from pictures and other props (e.g., Elley 1989; Huttenlocher 1991; Hart & Risley 1995; Weizman & Snow 2001; Hoff & Naigles 2002). The complexity of the sentence structure in the adult talk that children hear also affects their development (Huttenlocher et al. 2002; Vasilyeva, Huttenlocher, & Waterfall 2006). Longer sentences often contain information about words that might be new to a child (e.g., "Oh, that rabbit is soft and furry, just like our kitten. But the

Table 1.1	Math vocabulary
Category	**Examples**
numbers and quantities	*one, two three* (and so on); *a few, some half, many, most, almost all, all*
comparisons	*bigger, smaller, taller, shorter, longer, younger, older, thicker, thinner, faster, slower, more than, less than, as many as, equal to*
spatial/location	*next to, beside, behind, in front of, under, on top of, above, below, near, between*
math operations	*add, combine, subtract, separate, divide*
ordering/sequencing	*first, second, third, next, last, before, after*
time	*yesterday, tomorrow, last week, next week, soon, in a little while, a long time ago, morning, noon, night, early, late*

Based on Charlesworth & Lind (2003). For more on math vocabulary, see Greenes, Ginsburg, & Balfanz (2004).

rabbit's ears are longer and it has bigger feet, too, doesn't it?"). Good stories often contain relatively sophisticated vocabulary and syntax. If this, along with the teacher's own language and support, is considered, the potential for story reading to benefit children's oral language development is even greater.

◆ ◆ ◆

When teachers read stories to children, care must be taken not to undermine narrative comprehension. In the next few chapters, examples of storybook readings show how powerful instruction in narrative comprehension and language development can bolster learning in literacy, language, and mathematics without compromising any one area.

2

Reading *Inch by Inch:*
Effective Integration in Action

This chapter shows effective integration in action across content domains, imagining one preschool teacher's three readings of Leo Lionni's *Inch by Inch*. It demonstrates how teachers can support learning in mathematics, oral language, and literacy during story time. As we follow Ms. Freeman, our teacher, we see integration and robust instruction—and how it changes—over multiple readings of the same book. As previously discussed, an ineffective approach to integrating math with oral language and literacy is simply to use the story as a jumping-off point for a math activity. In this chapter, we see how in-depth, powerful instruction can maximize children's learning in all three domains.

The first reading

During the first reading, Ms. Freeman introduces the book and its ideas, and the children gain a basic understanding of the story. Note the teacher's comments; they are especially important to the children's comprehension of the narrative.

Introducing the story

Recall from Chapter 1, *Inch by Inch* is about an inchworm's cleverness in escaping from the birds that want to eat him. On the book's cover, the inchworm is perched atop a tall leaf, surrounded by many other leaves. Knowing that preschoolers are likely to have some difficulty in locating this small, green creature amid the green leaves, Ms. Freeman points to the tiny inchworm and asks, "What do you see here?" A few children reply that they see a caterpillar. Ms. Freeman confirms that there is indeed a caterpillar on the cover, and adds that this kind of caterpillar is called an inchworm. She then explains the approximate length of an inch by holding her thumb and index finger a short distance apart: "An inch is about this long, and that's about the size of the little caterpillar, isn't it?" The children nod in agreement.

Next, she reads the book's title, underlining each word as she reads it. "*Inch by Inch*. That's an interesting title, isn't it?" Continuing on, Ms. Freeman reads the name of the author and artist, then introduces the book by providing a very basic overview of the plot:

> I won't tell you everything that happens in the story, only that the inchworm is in danger because some birds think he would make a tasty dinner. But this inchworm is very clever—he can think fast and has good ideas. Let's read the story and find out what happens.

Reading the story

On the first page of the story, the inchworm is perched on the branch of a tree. A robin is sitting on a branch nearby, its open beak positioned near the inchworm. Ms. Freeman, with a concerned look on her face, shows the children the illustration.

Ms. Freeman: Oh, my! This looks like a dangerous situation for the little inchworm. Do you see that bird's beak? It's wide open, isn't it?

Children: Yes.

Ms. Freeman: And we know that birds like to eat caterpillars, don't we?

Ana: They get 'em with their mouths.

Ms. Freeman: Yes, birds catch caterpillars with their beaks, and then they eat them. I wonder what this robin has in mind. Let's read more and find out.

She reads the text, which states that the robin was hungry when he spotted the inchworm, and wants to "gobble him up."

"Gobble him up" means that the robin was about to eat him very quickly, very fast. It sounds to me like the robin is very hungry. Does it sound that way to you?

Michelle: I hope he doesn't do it.

Ana: Is he going to eat him?

Sam: Run away now!

Ms. Freeman: Well, I hope the robin doesn't eat the little inchworm. But I'm afraid he might. The robin's beak is so close to the little inchworm, and we know he's hungry. Let's read more and see what happens.

Next, we see the inchworm on a different branch, farther away from the robin, whose beak is now closed. Some children notice right away that the inchworm has not been eaten.

Jamie: He's still there!

Rashid: The bird didn't eat him!

Sam: Get away!

Ms. Freeman points to the inchworm, confirming the children's observations.

Ms. Freeman: I hope it's the *same* little inchworm, and not a *different* one. When we saw the inchworm on the last page, he was up here on this branch.

She points to the branch and turns back to the previous page to help children connect the two illustrations.

I'm a little worried that the robin might have eaten the inchworm we see here [points back to the previous page]. Let's read more and see if we can find out what's happening.

The story's next page informs us that, indeed, this is the very same inchworm as before. Now he is pleading with the robin not to eat him, saying that the robin should let him live because he is useful—he knows how to measure things. At first, the robin is skeptical of the inchworm's claim and demands that he prove it by measuring the robin's tail.

Ms. Freeman continues to read the text with expression, capturing the inchworm's concern and fear, as well as his pluck and positive outlook. She also captures the robin's dismissive, demanding attitude. After reading this, she continues her discussion with the children.

Ms. Freeman: Well, this is the same inchworm that we saw at the beginning of the story. He's a pretty quick thinker, isn't he? He has an idea for why the robin should not eat him. But I'm not sure the robin thinks that inchworms can measure things. He's going to make the inchworm show him, by measuring his tail. I sure hope the inchworm can do it, don't you?

Sam: Measure? Only people measure.

Ms. Freeman: Well, you might be right. Let's read more and see what that inchworm has in mind. I hope something works. If it doesn't, I'm worried that the robin will gobble him up. Remember, the book said that the robin was hungry.

Next, the inchworm responds to the robin's demand by using his body to measure the robin's tail, counting aloud as he measures. The single image on this page shows the inchworm on the robin's tail, measuring (see illustration).

Preschool children may not understand much about measurement, especially that it involves repetition of a unit. Thinking this might be a new concept, Ms. Freeman points to the very tip of the robin's tail and runs her finger along it toward the robin's back, stopping on the inchworm. While

The inchworm measuring the robin's tail, from *Inch by Inch.*

doing so, she explains more about measurement.

Ms. Freeman: The little inchworm started measuring at the tip of the robin's tail, way back here [places her finger on the tip of the robin's tail], and then he scrunched up and stretched out five times to reach the robin's back [traces the inchworm's path with her finger]. We see him here, bending his body to bring his tail-end up toward his head [points to his head]. After bending his body like this, he moves his head forward again to stretch out his body before he bends himself another time.

That's how an inchworm moves his body, and that's how he used it to measure the robin's tail. He started here at the tip [points to the tail again] and inched his way to where the robin's tail meets his back. So, the inchworm really can measure things. That's pretty amazing, isn't it?

Luis: Yes.

Sarah: He's pretty smart.

Jason: The robin looks mad.

Ms. Freeman: Maybe the robin is mad. It's hard to tell how a bird is feeling, because birds' faces are not like ours. They don't smile or change their faces like we do. The inchworm has measured the tail,

as the robin requested. But maybe he's mad, or at least sad, because he might be thinking now that he can't eat the little worm, because he's proved himself useful.

Remember? The robin is very hungry, and if he doesn't eat this caterpillar, he'll need to find something else for his dinner. Well, let's read more, and maybe we'll find out whether the robin is mad about something.

Ms. Freeman continues the story, expressively capturing the robin's delight in finding out the length of his tail. The children learn that the robin is enthusiastic about sharing the little worm's talent with some of his bird friends. Ms. Freeman reads through the next few pages, commenting after reading each one.

As she reads, the children voice agreement or add their own ideas, and Ms. Freeman responds briefly to each comment. When the text describes how the inchworm measures a hummingbird's whole body, she asks the children whether they think it took him very long to do this. They all agree that it didn't, because the hummingbird's body is so short.

The story continues on until a nightingale asks the inchworm to measure her song.

Ms. Freeman: Measure her song? How can the inchworm do that?

Ana: I don't know.

Sam: He can't do that!

Keisha: Maybe he can.

Ms. Freeman: The nightingale says, "Measure my song or I'll eat you for breakfast." Oh my. It looks like the inchworm is in danger, once again. I hope he can come up with another good idea, don't you?

Keisha: He should jump off the leaf!

Luis: He should measure some part of the nightingale's body.

Jason: His robin friend should come back and save him.

Ms. Freeman: Well, let's see what happens. [She reads the last line on the page.] "Then the inchworm had an idea."

She pauses to let the children wonder what his idea could be. Then she reads the text on the next page.

"'I'll try,' he said, 'go ahead and sing.'"

She reads the rest of the story without any comments, as she plans to discuss the ending with the children after she's finished. As she reads, she points to the inchworm on each page to help children locate him as he makes his escape.

Discussing the story

After finishing the book, Ms. Freeman returns to the page where the nightingale began to sing, and the inchworm began to move away.

Ms. Freeman: [She points to the inchworm.] Did you notice the direction the inchworm was moving?

Luis: Down. [He points down with his finger.] He was getting away from the bird.

Ms. Freeman: Yes, he was getting away from the nightingale. He didn't want the nightingale to eat him, did he?

She turns the page. The inchworm is pictured on the ground, hidden beneath a plant's leaves.

Why didn't the inchworm crawl from the top of one leaf to the top of the next leaf [points across several leaves in the illustration] as he escaped from the nightingale? Why did he crawl on the ground instead? [She points to the inchworm on the ground.]

Sarah: He would fall off the leaf.

Ana: He lives in the ground.

Ms. Freeman: He might have fallen off, but caterpillars have feet that hold on tightly when they are crawling. I don't think inchworms live in the ground. Earthworms do, but I don't think caterpillars do. We can get a book about that and find out.

I was thinking that the inchworm thought that the nightingale would not see him on the ground if she opened her eyes, because he'd be underneath all of the plants. He was quite clever again. He was a very smart inchworm, wasn't he?

Jason: He is a smart worm. He has good ideas.

Ana: Maybe he knows an earthworm that will let him come into his house.

Ms. Freeman: Yes, he was a smart little worm. And maybe he did think he might meet a friendly earthworm down there on the ground. I also was thinking at first that it would be impossible for the little inchworm to measure a song, and I thought surely the nightingale would eat him.

I thought the inchworm might just crawl up and down the same leaf, until the nightingale finished singing. I thought the inchworm might say, "Your song was ten trips up and down the leaf." I was thinking about how sometimes, when we're cooking as a class, we count the number of stirs so we know when it's someone else's turn with the spoon. Or, remember when I fried pancakes in an electric skillet one day at circle time, and you counted how long before I flipped the pancake over?

Rashid: Yes! It took to ten to cook the pancakes.

Ms. Freeman: That's right. We all counted to ten while the pancake cooked on one side. Then I flipped the pancake to the other side, and we counted to ten again while that side cooked. Then, I removed that pancake from the skillet and poured more batter in to make another pancake. Then we counted again. We kept doing that until all of the pancakes were cooked.

Well, that's what I thought the inchworm would do to measure the nightingale's song. I thought he might count the number of times that he could go up and down a leaf before the song ended. But the inchworm was very clever, and he escaped instead. What a clever inchworm. He outsmarted two predators. He thought of ways to keep them from eating him, didn't he?

The second reading

Ms. Freeman reads the book again the next day. A repeat reading of a storybook differs from the first. The children have a basic knowledge of the story, so the teacher can make more comments and ask subtler questions, deepening the children's understanding. The teacher also can respond more fully to what the children say, since the children will be able to pick up again after departing from the story reading. Their knowledge of the plot provides a framework that children hold onto during more extended discussions in a second or third reading. They can take in more information than is possible in a first reading, when they do not yet know the story.

Ms. Freeman reads the text selectively, leaving out things that the children understood easily the first time. This, too, makes it possible to have more discussion without extending story time beyond preschoolers' attention capacity.

To start the second reading, Ms. Freeman opens the book directly to the first page.

Ms. Freeman: I think you probably remember what the robin was thinking here.

Maria: "I'm gonna eat him."

Jamie: He was hungry.

Keisha: "I'm looking for dinner."

Ms. Freeman: Right, the book says that the robin was hungry and was thinking of gobbling up the inchworm he saw. What happened next?

For the most part, the teacher follows this approach throughout the second reading of the book. Using the illustrations, Ms. Freeman asks children to recall the events of the story. She listens carefully to children's comments and questions. She responds to affirm comments, to clarify points of confusion, or to add more information. Ms. Freeman and the children sometimes discuss the inchworm's thoughts and also the behavior and motivations of some of the birds. Sometimes, Ms. Freeman reads portions of the text to answer children's questions, or to confirm what a child has recalled. Since this book is so richly illustrated, Ms. Freeman can refer to details in the pictures, and she does this rather than read a lot of the text.

As the children comment, Ms. Freeman notices some misunderstandings. When this happens, Ms. Freeman helps children notice relevant details and provides additional information. She models *inferential thinking* (which involves reasoning and piecing together information to arrive at a conclusion), then supports children as they do the same. One misunderstanding arose when she reached a page showing a flamingo:

Rashid: Is that a snake?

Ms. Freeman: The inchworm does look like a little snake. But he's actually not a snake, because he doesn't have scaly skin. He's soft. The inchworm is a caterpillar, a baby insect, and someday, he will turn into a moth or a butterfly.

Rashid: No, I mean the pink thing.

Ms. Freeman: Oh, you mean the flamingo's neck? You think the flamingo's long neck looks like a snake?

Rashid: Yes.

Ms. Freeman: Well, it does look somewhat like a snake. For one thing, we don't see its whole body, so we don't see its legs and feet. Without the flamingo's legs and feet showing, I can see why you might think it looks like a snake.

Sarah: Snakes don't have beaks.

Ms. Freeman: That's right. Only birds have beaks. That's a very good clue for figuring out that this is a bird and not a snake. But I do agree that the flamingo's neck is shaped a lot like a snake, long and thin and winding around.

Keisha: It's definitely a flamingo. Birds have feathers, and snakes don't.

Ms. Freeman: That's true, and back here [turns back to a previous page where the robin was flying with the inchworm riding on his back] the book says that the robin and the inchworm "flew to where other birds needed to be measured." So, that helped me know that a flamingo was a bird. I also read about flamingos in a bird book, and I saw a picture of one.

But you are right, Rashid, it's a little difficult to tell in the illustration that the flamingo's neck is covered in feathers. The coloring and pattern almost make it look like a snake's skin.

Sarah: But it's not.

Ms. Freeman: No, it's not. Not with that big beak. And we also know that the robin was going to take the inchworm to measure other birds—not snakes.

During this reading, the teacher is able to reinforce key vocabulary in a natural way. On the page where the inchworm measures the flamingo's neck, the teacher says, "Oh, here is the flamingo, a bright pink bird. What part of the flamingo's body did the inchworm measure?" Ms. Freeman uses the word *flamingo* several times in the exchange about the bird's neck. She uses the bird's name in context, allowing children to hear it repeatedly and to try saying it themselves.

Ms. Freeman uses the same basic approach, as the class examines each page.

Ms. Freeman: Oh, here's the toucan with its very long and colorful beak. Here's the little inchworm, almost at the end of the toucan's beak. Where do you think the inchworm was when he started to measure the toucan's beak?

Michelle: Way up there. By his eye.

Ms. Freeman draws her finger down the line separating the toucan's head from its beak.

Ms. Freeman: It looks like the toucan's beak starts right here. I think you are right that the inchworm would have started way up here by its eye. But we don't really know, do we? Perhaps his friend the robin dropped him onto the middle of the toucan's beak, and he's now crawling down to its tip to start measuring from there. We don't really know, because we only see the inchworm this one time, right here, almost at the tip of the toucan's beak.

Michelle: He's already almost done, because he started up at the toucan's eye.

Ms. Freeman: Probably, although it's hard to know for sure. I think it might have been safer to start at the tip of the toucan's beak and end up at its eye, because if he went the other way he'd finish at the end of the beak and the toucan could easily gobble him up. The picture doesn't show us, and the book doesn't say where he started.

Discussing the story the second time

The reconstruction of the story took about 15 minutes and involved a lot of discussion. When the teacher reached the end of the book, she posed a question to prompt another brief discussion:

Ms. Freeman: We talked about how clever the inchworm was in this story, but we haven't talked about a character that was not very clever. When you look at this picture of the nightingale, do you see something that makes you think that the nightingale was not very clever?

Jason: She's not watching.

Maria: She closed her eyes. She didn't pay attention.

Ms. Freeman: Right. She wasn't watching, which meant she wasn't paying attention. Do you think the story might have ended differently if the nightingale had kept her eyes open while singing?

Sam: Yes.

Jason: No.

Sam: She might have eaten him.

The third reading

Two days later, Ms. Freeman reads the book again. This time, she reads the story without pausing much for discussion, because by now the children know the story very well and are not puzzled about the characters or their actions. The book's sparse text and simple illustrations make it easy and enjoyable for them to read along or chime in during their favorite parts.

Ms. Freeman points to the parts of the birds the inchworm measures, which helps children to recall the body parts named in the text. And to prepare the children for an activity she has planned to follow this reading, she comments in a way that directs their attention to details that will be relevant to the activity. She comments on the length of each body part; for example, she says, "Flamingos have very long necks. I can understand why a flamingo would ask the inchworm to measure its neck." Then, during the activity, Ms. Freeman will share pictures of other birds, and the children will discuss which parts of the birds' bodies would be best for an inchworm to measure.

Extending the learning

The teacher uses information books to add to the children's knowledge of the birds featured in the story and to get them to think about the body parts of other birds. This allows for more math learning, as well as more language and literacy learning. Ms. Freeman uses the book *Eye Wonder: Birds*, by Samantha Gray and Sarah Walker, to find information about the length of the toucan's beak in relation to its total body length. Ms. Freeman shares this information about the toucan's beak, as well as general information about the bird, with the children. She also uses a large picture of the toucan in the book to explain the meaning of some of the information; for example, she shows the children how "the toucan's beak is about one-third the length of its whole body."

This book shows several manakin birds alongside the toucan, and Ms. Freeman compares their very short beaks with the very large beak of the toucan. She wonders out loud whether a manakin's beak is even one inchworm long. She tells the class that if the inchworm were to measure one of these beaks, he might announce, "Your beak is just half an inchworm long."

This discussion exposes children to informational text and provides interesting details about birds. Ms. Freeman also uses the activity to introduce children to additional measurement concepts, such as weight. The children learn that even though the toucan's beak is large, it is light and not heavy, because it is hollow. Ms. Freeman explains that "*light* means not very heavy" and that "*hollow* means empty inside, not solid." To support these explanations, she shows a drinking straw ("It's empty inside, hollow") and also a cylindrical block ("This cylindrical block is solid, not hollow, which makes it kind of heavy, not light"). She tells the children that both the straw and the block will be available during center time for them to hold and feel the difference in their weights. Then Ms. Freeman shows pictures of birds' beaks in a few other suitable information books: for example, *Beaks!* by Sneed Collard; *Unbeatable Beaks*, by Stephen Swinburne; and the National Audubon Society's *Birds: First Field Guide*.

After reviewing pictures of birds featured in *Inch by Inch* and discussing the birds' great choices of body parts for the inchworm to measure, Ms. Freeman shows a few additional birds from the information books and asks the children to think further about which of those bird's body parts might be the best for an inchworm to measure. For example, after Ms. Freeman shows a picture of an owl in *Eye Wonder*, she says, "Look at the enormous wingspan of this owl. The book says, 'Their prey may not even hear them approach as they swoop down to sink in their talons.'" Ms. Freeman then briefly explains the meaning of the words *wingspan*, *prey*, and *talon*.

She is careful not to include too much in one discussion, or to extend story time beyond 20 minutes, even though the children are highly engaged. The teacher tells the children that these books about birds will be available in the library during center time. Another book, about caterpillars (*Caterpillar,* by Karen Hartley, Chris MacRo, and Philip Taylor), will be there, too, as will *Inch by Inch.*

At the very end of the discussion, Ms. Freeman tells the children that tomorrow they will break into small groups and use Popsicle sticks and short pieces of string to measure some of their own body parts. They will also use their fingers to measure various objects.

◆　◆　◆

The next chapter will revisit in more detail the techniques and strategies that Ms. Freeman uses during these readings of *Inch by Inch,* and discusses several other examples of rich instruction surrounding storybooks. All of the examples in Chapter 3 will again illustrate how well-planned instruction can effectively integrate learning in mathematics, language, and literacy.

Reflection questions

1. In what ways did Ms. Freeman consider the children's prior knowledge as she began the first reading of *Inch by Inch*? As she conducted the second and third readings, how did she adjust the discussion to match children's interests and clear up misunderstandings?

2. Would her approach have worked in your classroom? What alternative techniques could she have used?

3. How did Ms. Freeman ensure that introducing the concept of measurement did not compromise the children's comprehension of the story?

4. Which domain does she emphasize the most—language, literacy, or mathematics? How could she have modified the readings if she had decided to emphasize a different domain?

3

Strategies to Enhance Learning During and After Story Time

In the last chapter, we saw an example of effective integrated instruction as Ms. Freeman read the book *Inch by Inch* to children during story time. In this chapter, we will analyze the techniques and strategies Ms. Freeman used during that reading, as well as during readings of two other books, *Caps for Sale* and *The Puddle Pail*. Her practice demonstrates how mathematics, oral language, and various literacy skills can all be addressed in the course of reading a story.

The balance in attention to mathematics versus language and literacy will of course differ depending on each book's basic plot and on the teacher's intended emphasis. With the prominence of measurement in its story, *Inch by Inch* allows a teacher to focus more on a math concept than might be the case with many other books. Still, even with this mathematics-rich book, the first reading focused primarily on the themes of the book, using the mathematics focus to deepen children's understanding of the themes in subsequent readings. The teacher's explanation to the children of how the inchworm measured the robin's tail illustrates genuine integration of mathematics, language, and literacy instruction, benefiting children's learning in each domain.

Before we begin our analysis, it will be helpful to summarize the plots of the other two narratives

we will discuss in this chapter. In *Caps for Sale*, by Esphyr Slobodkina, a peddler carrying a stack of caps on the top of his head walks out to the country to take a rest. He finds a tree to sit under and then falls asleep. Upon waking, he realizes that his stack of caps is no longer on his head—all that's left is his own cap. He discovers that monkeys sitting above him on the branches of the tree are wearing them. The peddler tells the monkeys to give back his caps, and accompanies each demand with a movement of his hands or feet. Rather than return his caps, however, the monkeys merely imitate the peddler's actions. After many failed attempts to get his caps back, the peddler gives up. In anger, he takes off his cap and throws it to the ground. The monkeys do the same, and the peddler gathers the caps that rain down around him.

In *The Puddle Pail*, by Elisa Kleven, the main characters are two crocodile brothers. Each carries a pail to the beach, and each has a unique idea about what to collect in his pail. Sol, the older brother, collects items such as shells, rocks, and feathers. Ernst, the younger brother, is attracted to clouds, stars, and cookies—things that are fascinating and beautiful, but not easy to collect. Despite Sol's advice, Ernst decides to collect puddles with pretty reflections in them. Of course, the reflections disappear as soon as Ernst scoops the puddles into his pail. In the end, Ernst paints pictures of all the reflections he tried to collect.

One of Ms. Freeman's key strategies is reading each book multiple times. Research tells us that children understand the story more deeply each time a book is read to them (Morrow 1987). For example, with each successive reading, children verbalize more associations and make more interpretative comments. Each reading of the book serves a different purpose; together, multiple readings are highly effective in maximizing children's learning.

Now let's revisit in more detail the teaching strategies Ms. Freeman used in the last chapter with *Inch by Inch* and will now use with the two additional narratives.

Before the first reading: Steps to introduce the book

Before the first reading of a book, there is an important window of opportunity both to provide key information to children and to set the tone of the reading.

Introducing a storybook to preschoolers can be thought of as a short series of steps. Depending on the book, the order of steps one and two might be reversed. But the steps are listed below in the order Ms. Freeman used them:

1. Show the cover and consider with the children what the book might be about. The very first thing Ms. Freeman did before reading *Inch by Inch* was hold the book up so that the children could see the picture on the front cover. Next, she pointed out the tiny figure of the inchworm and asked the children to identify it. She discussed it briefly and demonstrated how long it was with her fingers.

2. Read the cover and track its words with a finger—Ms. Freeman read, "*Inch by Inch,* by Leo Lionni."

3. Very briefly sum up the basic plot or main themes of the book—without giving away too much information—and lead into the book with a statement: "Let's read the story and find out what happens."

Ms. Freeman did all of this in just a few minutes.

Some books have an unusual or detailed image on the cover that might need a little extra discussion. Before Ms. Freeman reads the book *The Puddle Pail*, the class spends some time talking about what they see on the cover and what they think might be happening. Ms. Freeman is careful to point to each image on the cover as they discuss it. To start, Ms. Freeman identifies the two crocodiles pictured on the book's cover. She also draws the children's attention to two things central to the story—the colorful water in the pail and the rainbow in the sky overhead, which will combine in the story to form a reflection.

Ms. Freeman: We see two crocodiles here on the book's cover. One is holding a pail, which is another name for a bucket, and inside it is colorful water. Do you see that?

Children: Yes.

Ms. Freeman: I also see a rainbow in the sky overhead, and I think the colors in the water are a reflection of the rainbow. Look at the rainbow and at the water in the pail and see whether you think the colors look the same.

Jamie: I see it.

Increasing the Power of Instruction

Sarah: I see some yellow in it.

Jamie: It's the same.

Ms. Freeman: Oh, yes, I see the yellow too, right here in the middle. And then, down here in the pail, I see the yellow band of the rainbow again. See that?

Children: Yes.

Ms. Freeman: There's also an orange band of color in the rainbow, up here at the top, and also one in the bucket. Look right here. See it?

Luis: Yes.

Jamie: I do. It looks red.

Ms. Freeman: It does look a little reddish orange in the pail. The rainbow in the pail is what is called a *reflection*. The real rainbow is up in the sky. But the water in the pail is like a mirror, and we can see the rainbow's reflection in it.

Maria: I see it. Cool.

Ms. Freeman: Now let's look for a minute at the crocodiles' faces. The green one looks a little angry to me. See that?

Jamie: He looks mean.

Maria: He wants the rainbow in the bucket.

Sarah: Maybe it's his turn to hold the bucket.

Ms. Freeman: Maybe, or maybe he doesn't think the reflection is pretty. But the blue crocodile has a kind of happy, satisfied expression on his face, doesn't he? I'm thinking that maybe he likes the reflection.

Sarah: It's his turn to hold it.

Ms. Freeman: Maybe. Or maybe he's happy for some other reason. Let's read the story and see what happens. Before I start reading the story, I'll read the title, *The Puddle Pail,* and the author's name, Elisa Kleven. [She underlines the print with her finger as she reads the words.]

Mmmm. That's an interesting title. I guess maybe the water in the pail was scooped up from a puddle. Okay, let's see what happens to these two crocodiles.

With other books, the title itself might be difficult for preschoolers to comprehend. One such book is *Caps for Sale*, the full title of which is *Caps for Sale: A Tale of a Peddler, Some Monkeys, and Their*

Monkey Business. When introducing this book, Ms. Freeman makes sure to explain what "monkey business" means. While she could also discuss what "peddler" means, she chooses to wait so as not to overwhelm the children with too much information before beginning the book. Also, in this initial discussion with the children, the idea of "monkey business" is more complex and thus more important to explain.

While showing the cover and introducing the story, she points out the man with a cap in his hand, sleeping in the tree. She also points to the stack of caps on the ground, in front of the tree, and to the two monkeys peeking out from behind the tree's trunk. She then reads the main title, *Caps for Sale*, and then the subtitle, *A Tale of a Peddler, Some Monkeys, and Their Monkey Business,* and the author's name. Doing this provides a good jumping-off point for Ms. Freeman to explain,

> "Monkey business" means playing tricks on someone, or getting into mischief. When someone "gets into mischief," they do something that bothers other people.

To finish the introduction, she says,

> I think the monkeys we see here probably do something in the story that bothers this man. Let's read the story and find out what happens.

The first reading: Strategies and techniques

The first reading of the book is critical to children's understanding of the narrative. The main purpose of this reading is to foster comprehension of these story components:

- *Characters*. Who are the main characters, and what are they like?

- *Theme*. Is there a theme, such as friendship?

- *Ideas*. What are the main ideas, opinions, and thoughts expressed? (For example, if the book's theme is friendship, what ideas are expressed about friendship?)

- *Plot*. What actually happens?

Using comprehension asides

How does a teacher get through the first reading of a book and help children comprehend the story without getting bogged down in long discussions about what is happening? As discussed in Chapter 1, teachers can use *comprehension asides* to convey key information. In this approach, the teacher conveys essential information as she thinks and wonders aloud about a character or situation. Sometimes questions are posed to the children, and children often comment spontaneously, as well. The questions the teacher poses are not intended to prompt lengthy discussions. The teacher is also careful to respond to children's spontaneous comments in ways that do not interrupt the story for long.

Below is an example from a first reading of *Caps for Sale*. Ms. Freeman has just read the section in the story where the peddler awakens from a nap only to find that his caps are gone. Pay particular attention to Ms. Freeman's use of the phrases "I'm noticing," "I wonder," and "I think."

Ms. Freeman: I'm noticing something different about the peddler now. Do you see something that has changed?

Michelle: His eyes are open.

Ms. Freeman: Yes, he is awake now; his eyes are open. There's also something else I'm noticing that is different about the peddler. Something has changed since he sat down to take his nap.

Michelle: The hats are gone.

Ms. Freeman: Yes, they are. I wonder what happened to them?

She turns back to an earlier page where the peddler is shown sitting against the tree with the tall stack of caps on his head. She points to the caps on the peddler's head.

> He had a lot of hats on his head, back here, when he sat down under the tree. [She returns to the page where the peddler has just awakened.] But now they are all gone.

Keisha: What happened to them? Where'd they go?

Ms. Freeman: I think we'll find out when we read more of the story. I don't think the peddler has noticed yet that his caps are gone, do you?

Children: No.

Ms. Freeman: I wonder when he will realize that his caps are gone?

Keisha: He'll be sad.

Ms. Freeman: Probably, and maybe mad too. Let's read more and see what happens. [She reads the next page.] Well, now the peddler realizes that his caps are missing. I think that he's probably wondering what happened to them, and I think he's probably going to look for them, because those caps are very important to the peddler, aren't they?

Sam: He wants to buy lunch.

Jamie: They were pretty colors.

Ms. Freeman: Yes, he needs to sell the caps to earn money, to buy lunch and other things. And the caps were pretty, all different colors. Well, let's see what the peddler does now. I sure hope he finds his caps, don't you?

Using direct clarification

Occasionally teachers will need to give direct information during the first reading to clarify the text and explain unknown words. For instance, Ms. Freeman explains what *peddler* means after reading the first page of *Caps for Sale*, where the peddler is introduced:

> A peddler is someone who goes from house to house to sell things. See, he's not inside a store. He's walking through the village to sell his caps.

Similarly, during the first reading of *The Puddle Pail*, she provides explanations of words that she thinks are unfamiliar to the children. For example, she explains that a *collection* consists of many items that are slightly different but are of the same kind, such as a group of different rocks or a bunch of different feathers. Then she explains that a person adds new items to a collection as time goes on, and that people often like to look at their collections and show them to other people. She also explains that making collections is a *hobby* for some people, something they do for fun.

Providing useful explanations for words in books as they are encountered helps children learn more word meanings than if the teacher simply reads the book without discussing vocabulary (Elley 1989; Beck, McKeown, & Kucan 2002; Collins 2004).

Mathematics integration during the first reading

As stated above, the main focus of the first reading is on the basic components of the story. It's very important to focus on children's narrative comprehension at this stage, and therefore there is less math-related discussion unless it directly helps with narrative comprehension.

As we saw in Chapter 2, when Ms. Freeman introduced *Inch by Inch,* she did not provide a technical explanation of an inch, nor did she show a ruler. A technical understanding of an inch is not necessary to comprehend the story. Taking time for such an explanation would have delayed the story reading, which can decrease children's attention, interest, and ultimately their overall comprehension. Moreover, the story is not really about inches or measurement—it is about using ideas to outsmart enemies. Thus, providing a technical explanation of an inch might have focused children's attention on an unnecessary level of detail and pushed their thinking down a path unrelated to the main theme of the story.

Though young children themselves tend to veer off on tangents unrelated to a story (Neuman 1990; Beck & McKeown 2001), adults should not encourage a focus on marginally related ideas. Rather, in their own comments and in their gentle responses to children's comments, they should help children regain their focus on the text (Beck & McKeown 2001).

However, the concept of measurement *is* important to the overall story, and Ms. Freeman did need to bring it up during the first reading of *Inch by Inch* to introduce the concept to the children. When she did so, she focused on the basic idea that the inchworm measured the robin's tail with his body. Her explicit description of what actually transpired when the inchworm measured the robin's tail helped to convey the basic concept of unit repetition to the children, without relying on a technical explanation. This basic understanding

of a mathematical concept was reinforced and strengthened during the later two readings of the book.

In contrast, during the first reading of *Caps for Sale,* Ms. Freeman mentions math content only in a very general way, rather than in relation to a very specific concept such as measurement. For example, Ms. Freeman states that the peddler "had a lot of caps to sell," that "the stack on his head was very high," and that "he had a lot of hats on his head," but now "they are all gone." Similarly, during the first reading of *The Puddle Pail* she does not count items shown in the illustrations, except for one instance when Sol returns to Ernst with a pail full of items. Here, the text specifies the number of each item ("Twelve seashells, eight feathers . . . "), and Ms. Freeman questions Sol's motivation for telling Ernst precisely how many of each item he has collected.

In the first readings of each of these books, any focus on math-related content is in support of the children's overall understanding of the story's basic theme, events, or characters.

Discussing the book afterwards

An important strategy to aid comprehension is discussing the story after reading it (Morrow 1987; Collins 2004). Discussions following the reading of a story not only bolster children's understanding of the sequence of events, but they also deepen children's understanding of characters' feelings, motivations, and behavior. An emphasis on "why" questions helps children with the reflective, analytical thinking required to comprehend narratives (Dickinson & Smith 1994; Teale & Martinez 1996; Collins 2004). One way to set up such questions is to flip back to the page or pages where important plot changes occur. For example, after reading *Inch by Inch,* Ms. Freeman returned to where the inchworm escapes from the nightingale. She asked the children why he may have chosen his method of escape.

After reading *Caps for Sale,* Ms. Freeman revisits the pages where the peddler tries to reclaim his caps. She reviews the sequence of the peddler's attempts and the monkeys' reactions, and the children enjoy chiming in and acting out the words. Then, she prompts a reflective and somewhat challenging discussion:

Ms. Freeman: You know, now that I am thinking more about those monkeys, I shouldn't have been surprised that they threw their caps down when the peddler threw his. I should have expected it. There are some clues in the story that tell us that the monkeys probably would throw down their caps when the peddler threw his. Does anybody have an idea about the clues?

Rashid: What are they?

Sarah: What clues?

Ms. Freeman guides the children back through the relevant pages, to review the peddler's actions and the monkeys' reactions. She reminds them that the monkeys always did exactly what the peddler did—they imitated him.

Ms. Freeman: It makes sense, then, that the monkeys would throw their caps down when the peddler threw his down. Although monkeys cannot understand what people say, they can imitate what people do. They imitated everything else the peddler did, and when the peddler threw down his cap, the monkeys threw theirs down, too. Does that make sense to you?

Sarah: Yes.

Rashid: Yeah. That's why it happened.

Sarah: That was a good idea he had.

Ms. Freeman: I'm not sure the peddler did this on purpose. Remember, he had given up, and he just threw his cap down because he was mad. But I guess he discovered that it would work, after he did it.

The second reading: Strategies and techniques

The second reading of the story should take place within a few days of the first. During this reading, the teacher can now ask more questions and comment in ways that deepen the children's understanding. The teacher can also respond more particularly to the children's questions and reactions. The main purposes of this reading are to:

- reconstruct the narrative;
- reinforce knowledge gained from the story; and
- begin to build off of this knowledge to engage children in higher-level thinking.

Reconstructing with discussion and prompts

During the second reading, teachers can encourage children's recall of the story through the use of prompts. For example, in her second reading of *Inch by Inch*, Ms. Freeman prompted the children when she said, "I think you probably remember what the robin was thinking here." With this encouragement, the children shared their knowledge of the character's intentions and the story's plot up to that point.

Similarly, during the second reading of *Caps for Sale*, Ms. Freeman uses the prompt "Do you remember . . . ?" at several points. For example, when she turns to the page where we learn that the hungry peddler has sold no caps and has no money for lunch, she asks, "Do you remember what he decided to do?" Later on, when the peddler becomes so angry that he throws down his cap, Ms. Freeman prompts the children again:

Ms. Freeman: Do you remember what the peddler was thinking right here, when he threw his own cap down?

Ana: "I'm going home."

Jason: He wouldn't get his caps back from the monkeys.

Ms. Freeman: Yes, I think he had given up, and was ready to return home without his caps. He thought he'd never get his caps back. Remember, the book says that he "began to walk away." So that means he didn't expect to get his caps back. He had given up.

Keisha: But they gave them back.

Ms. Freeman: Yes, they did. But that was after they saw the peddler throw his own cap down. When the peddler threw his own cap down, he was probably thinking that he wouldn't get his caps back and that he might as well just go home. He had even started to walk away.

Keisha: Oh, yeah. I remember that.

Mathematics integration during the second reading

Since children have a basic understanding of the story from the first reading, the teacher can now include more math instruction, as doing so will no longer undermine children's story comprehension. Even here, however, the math instruction the teacher provides should deepen the children's understanding of the story.

For example, during the second reading of *The Puddle Pail*, Ms. Freeman suggests that the children count several of the collections featured in the book to find out how many items there are in each collection. First they examine Sol's rock and feather collections. They learn that there are 18 feathers and 25 rocks.

Rashid: He has more rocks.

Ms. Freeman: Yes, Sol does. Twenty-five is more than 18; you are right. So, he had more rocks than feathers. These are collections he already has, at home. And later he collects more rocks and feathers when he and Ernst are at the beach. [She flips ahead to find the pages.] He still finds more rocks than feathers. "Nineteen little rocks" [points to them] and "eight feathers" [points to them]. So, I'm thinking it was a lot easier to find rocks than it was to find feathers.

A few pages later Sol suggests to Ernst that he might want to collect cookies, and Ernst says that he wishes he could collect cookies in his stomach. At this point, Ms. Freeman wonders out loud, "How many cookies would Ernst have in his stomach if he ate all the cookies in the picture?" The picture depicts three rows of five cookies each, and Ms. Freeman suggests that the children help her count them. After they have been counted, Ms. Freeman comments that Ernst would have had quite a stomachache if he had eaten all fifteen cookies.

Several pages later, when Sol returns to show Ernst all the things he has collected in his pail, Ms. Freeman comments that a person who collects things often counts the items to determine how many there are. She explains that it's very difficult to count items when they are all mixed up in one container, as Sol's items are. To count the items,

she says, Sol probably spread them all out on the ground, and then sorted them into different groups:

> He looked at the items carefully, and decided which ones were rocks, which were feathers, which were seaweed, and which ones were not any of these things. This is how we see them here in the illustrations. [She points to the collections.] Then Sol counted the items in each group, which is how he knew he had found twelve seashells, eight feathers, nineteen little rocks, and three clumps of seaweed.

Ms. Freeman then reads the rest of the book, commenting at some points, and at others asking the children to recall some of the more important story events or to explain why a character behaved in a certain way. Her comments about sorting and grouping in particular help lay the groundwork for later math activities involving classification. Analyzing a collection and learning about classification is a form of data analysis, an important part of mathematics learning (NCTM 2000).

The primary purpose of the comments and ensuing discussions is to help children make sense of the story, although they also support mathematics learning.

Discussing the book afterwards

With some stories it may be effective to discuss math-related content after the second reading. For example, after finishing the second reading of *Caps for Sale*, Ms. Freeman leads the children in counting and in thinking about a mathematical question. She prompts discussion:

Ms. Freeman: I wonder how many monkeys are in the tree? It sure looks to me like there are a lot of them. Let's count them and see.

After leading the children in counting with her, she comments:

> I'm very glad there were just 16 monkeys and not 17. Do you know why I'm thinking that?

Jamie: There was already a lot.

Luis: Because they were mean.

Ms. Freeman: That's true, the monkeys were a little mean. There were also a lot of monkeys, enough to take all of the caps, except the peddler's own checked cap. There was just one cap left on his head. If there had been one more monkey, 17 instead of 16, would the peddler have had one cap left on his head?

Children: No.

Ms. Freeman: And if one cap had not been left on his head, let's think about what would have happened at the end. Would the peddler have had a cap to throw on the ground?

Children: No.

Ms. Freeman: And if he hadn't had a cap to throw down, would the monkeys ever have thrown their caps down?

Children: Yes . . . no . . .

Ms. Freeman: Maybe, but probably not. So that's why I'm really glad that there were only 16 monkeys, not 17.

Maria: And they are mean, too.

Ms. Freeman: Well, the peddler probably thought so. They did like to play tricks on the peddler; they were a little mischievous. Maybe that was mean when the caps were so very important to someone. But I don't think the monkeys understood that. They were probably just trying to have some fun. But the peddler didn't think it was much fun, did he?

Maria: No, they weren't nice. He was mad.

Ms. Freeman: Yes, he was.

As we can see, this math-related discussion segued naturally into a conversation about the characters' motivations and feelings.

Follow-up activities

In most situations, teachers will want to save follow-up math-related activities for after the third reading, but depending on the book and the children's prior knowledge, it may be appropriate to introduce an activity at this point.

Children might do such an activity in another area of the classroom, such as the math center, or in another learning context, such as during small group time. For example, after the second reading of *The Puddle Pail*, Ms. Freeman shows the children a collection of bottle caps, discusses how they might use it, and then suggests that the children explore the collection further during center time.

She explains that some of the caps came from milk bottles, some from bottles of juice, and others from bottles of soda. As she holds up a bottle cap, a child remembers part of the story:

Jason: They saw a bottle cap in that puddle.

Ms. Freeman opens the book again, turning to the page where Sol spots a cap and suggests that Ernst might like to collect caps.

Ms. Freeman: Yes, they did. But Ernst wasn't interested in the cap, was he? What did he see in the puddle instead?

She points to the reflections of items in the puddle.

Jason: Birds.

Michelle: Clouds.

Rashid: The blue sky.

Ms. Freeman: Yes, he saw reflections of things in the sky, and that's when he got the idea to collect puddles with their reflections. Well, I didn't find my bottle caps in puddles on the ground. I saved them at home, after I was finished with a bottle.

I'm going to put this collection of three kinds of bottle caps all together on one tray and put the tray over in the puzzles and manipulatives area. You might like to look at them, sort them, and count them during center time. And if you want to bring some milk caps or juice bottle caps from home, we can add them to our collection. I'll keep saving bottle caps, too.

The third reading: Strategies and techniques

The third reading of the story should take place within a few days of the second. This is a fluid reading, with much less commentary from the teacher than in the previous two readings. Children will often participate in the reading, especially if there is some portion of the text that is highly memorable. The main purposes of this reading are to:

- reinforce story comprehension (as before) and
- use the story as a jumping-off point to build further knowledge and enhance skills.

The third reading is often the most effective time to prompt math-related thinking and discussion, as the children should have a strong grasp of the narrative by this point (Morrow 1987).

Discussing the book afterwards

One effective strategy is to pose challenging questions to the children, such as questions that encourage children to consider how a small change in the story could have altered events. This is also a natural way to integrate math-related content.

For example, after reading *Caps for Sale* for the third time, Ms. Freeman leads the discussion with questions pertaining both to the events of the story and to the related mathematical components. She asks how the story might have unfolded if only four monkeys had visited the tree—instead of 16—and if each had taken just one cap. Her approach in this discussion is similar to that after the second reading, but the question she poses this time is a bit more challenging:

Ms. Freeman: Would the peddler have noticed that some caps were missing before arriving home and removing them from his head? What do you think?

Maria: He would have noticed.

San: No, he wouldn't think they were gone.

Ms. Freeman: If you think he would have noticed, tell me what you think would have made him notice. How would he have known they were gone?

Maria: Because he wouldn't have any red ones any more.

Ms. Freeman: Well, you are right that if there were only four monkeys in the tree, and if each took just one cap, all of the red ones would have been gone. [She opens the book to a relevant page and points to the red caps, which are on top.] See here? 1, 2, 3, 4. But how would he have known that they were gone?

Sarah: He couldn't feel them.

Ms. Freeman: He might have felt that the stack of caps wasn't as heavy, or noticed that the stack of caps wasn't as high if he reached up and checked his caps with his hand. That's one way that he might have found out. Does that make sense to everybody?

Children: Yes.

Follow-up activities

To further children's understanding, teachers can move on to planned activities after this reading. You may recall that during her third reading of *Inch by Inch*, Ms. Freeman made specific comments to prepare the children for a discussion activity focused on which parts of birds' bodies would be best for an inchworm to measure.

Similarly, after finishing their third reading of *The Puddle Pail*, Ms. Freeman shows the children some new classroom collections, which she relates to their previous discussions about the characters' collections and collecting in general. One is a collection of twist ties with metal wire down their middles, for use with the magnets in the science center. Another is a collection of junk mail envelopes, which the children can use in the writing center. A third is a collection of seashells for feeling, examining with a magnifying glass, and sorting by type (e.g., big, small, white, speckled). Ms. Freeman explains that she gathered the items for the children to use in the classroom, and that the collections of twist ties and envelopes are not permanent collections. But the group of shells, she says, is a permanent collection to which she will continue to add items.

Follow-up experiences are often introduced during story time, but are put into action during later periods such as center or small group time. This is an effective strategy to extend integrated learning throughout the day (and in different instructional contexts, which we will explore in Part II of this book). For example, after her third reading of *Caps for Sale*, Ms. Freeman introduces an activity that children can engage in later during center time. At the very end of their discussion of the book, the teacher turns to the page where the monkeys are sitting on a branch of the tree, each wearing a cap.

Ms. Freeman: I think I can figure out which monkeys got their caps first, which ones got their caps next, which ones got theirs after that, and which ones got their caps last. We don't have time to talk about this question right now.

But you might want to think about it later. I'm going to clip the book open and put it on this large tray. And I'm going to put a second copy of *Caps for Sale* on the tray with it, and put them all over on the puzzles and manipulatives table. If you want to think about which monkeys got their caps first, and then which ones got theirs next, and so on, you can look at the books over there later today, during center time. I'll be very curious to know what you think.

Promoting children's inferential thinking

Children's literacy learning is supported in a variety of ways during story reading, such as when a teacher helps children understand that a story text typically leaves unstated many things that the reader can infer. For example, when the inchworm in *Inch by Inch* measured the robin's tail, the brief text did not relate details about all of the inchworm's actions. Nor did the illustrations depict the inchworm's incremental progress. But Ms. Freeman talked with the children about what the inchworm was doing, and the children gained an understanding of his unstated actions.

Ms. Freeman supported inferential learning while reading the other two books, as well. During the third reading of *Caps for Sale*, the discussion led her to mention that the peddler had four caps in each color. When she asked the children to think about the order in which the monkeys got their caps, the children had to think about the order in which the different groups of colored hats were arranged on the peddler's head. This was a clever, effective way to get children to use information from the story to think about the unstated actions of a story's characters.

During the second reading of *The Puddle Pail*, Ms. Freeman wondered how many cookies were pictured and counted them with the children. Then, after counting, she commented that Ernst would have a stomachache if he ate this many cookies. This linked the information given in the text and illustration to a possible consequence for the character. Ms. Freeman also mentioned that Sol probably had to organize his collection of items on the ground so that he could count them, though the book does not include these intervening actions. By providing these details, the teacher taught the children that stories often do not tell us everything that a character does, and that we must draw inferences.

When there is an absence of detail about a story event, listeners or readers need to combine their prior knowledge with the information provided in the text. Using these two sources of information, they can infer that certain actions occurred that are not explicitly described or illustrated in the book. When a teacher provides explanations and statements that make his or her reasoning explicit, children learn about the kind of thinking required and see that they themselves must think while listening to a story. The teacher's explanations also provide opportunities for children to acquire knowledge, as their store of prior knowledge is much smaller than an adult's. Over time, children gradually acquire knowledge that will help them engage in inferential thinking.

Including different types of books

Children also benefit when teachers introduce different genres of books. When they see and hear texts written in different formats, children learn that there are differences among the structures of various kinds of texts. The little research that has been conducted on early exposure to information books shows that it benefits reading comprehension and leads to higher proficiency in writing of informational text in kindergarten and primary grades (Duke & Kays 1998; Casbergue & Plauche 2003; Duke, Pearson, & Taberski 2003). Using information books as well as narratives also increases interest for some children who prefer information books to other types of books (Caswell & Duke 1998; Jobe & Dayton-Sakari 2002).

Even when children's interest in books is already quite high, reading information books has strong benefits. For example, well-chosen information books expand children's knowledge of science and social studies, helping children develop background knowledge and vocabulary to draw upon in future learning experiences. Through descriptions, photographs, and illustrations, informational texts allow children to gain an understanding of things they have not or cannot experience directly. An opportunity for this kind of learning was provided when Ms. Freeman used information books about birds in the discussion following the third reading of *Inch by Inch*.

Focusing on vocabulary

Ms. Freeman used complex sentences in many of her explanations, such as when she described how the inchworm measured the robin's tail when reading *Inch by Inch*:

> The little inchworm started measuring at the tip of the robin's tail, way back here, and then he scrunched up and stretched out five times to reach the robin's back. . . . After bending his body like this, he moves his head forward again to stretch out his body before he bends himself another time.

The teacher's use of complex sentences helps build children's vocabularies and serves as a good model for children's syntactic and grammatical development (Hoff & Naigles 2002; Huttenlocher et al. 2002).

When she talked about the inchworm, Ms. Freeman supported children's oral vocabulary development: She used the word *tip* in relation to the robin's tail, *scrunched up* and *stretched out* in relation to the movements of the inchworm's body, and the directional word *forward*. A number of times, she also used the word *measure* and its variations in different contexts (e.g., *is measuring, to measure, can measure*).

Table 3.1

Examples of higher-level words used in teacher commentary

Caps for Sale

bothers	earns	mystery	shade
branches	except	noticing	support
clues	expect	peeking	trunk
decided	frustrated	realized	unusual
disappeared	imitate	removing	wondering
discovered	mischief	search	

The Puddle Pail

band	decide	impress	recognize
beautiful	easier	instead	reflection
bragging	exaggerating	interested	satisfied
colorful	expression	permanent	wondering

As was pointed out earlier, the teacher reinforced the birds' names as she and the children reconstructed the story in the second reading of *Inch by Inch*, and she helped children learn new vocabulary and facts about birds when she shared information books with them.

Also, when reading each of the three storybooks, Ms. Freeman's own language was rich in high-level vocabulary. The teacher's use of high-level vocabulary influences children's vocabulary development, especially in contexts where the words are explained in familiar terms and supported physically; for example, through the illustrations in a book (Weizman & Snow 2001). (For examples, see Table 3.1 on the previous page.)

Table 3.2

Examples of math-related words used during story readings

Below are examples of math-related words and phrases that a teacher might use when discussing these two books and introducing related activities. Many of these words are not used in the books themselves, but are incorporated by the teacher into the story reading to enhance children's mathematics learning.

	Caps for Sale	*The Puddle Pail*
Introduction to the Story		
cardinal number	"*two* monkeys peeking out from behind the tree"	"we see *two* crocodiles" "*one* is holding" "*one* in the bucket"
ordinal number		"I'll read the title *first*"
spatial location	"*in front* of the tree" "two monkeys peeking out from *behind* the tree" "*on the top* of his head"	"in the sky *overhead*" "in the *middle*" "*up* here *at the top*"
The First Reading and Discussion		
size and quantity	"*a lot* of caps to sell" "the stack on his head was *very high*" "let's read *more*"	"Sol has a *pretty big* rock collection" "his collection of string is *not very big*" "he has *quite a few* feathers" "let's count the rocks to see *how many* there really are" "are as *many . . . as*" "19 *little* rocks"
comparison	"something about him is not *the same* as it was"	"are *as many . . . as*"
number operations		"a person *adds* new items to a collection"
spatial location	"his caps are *up in* the tree" "a lot of monkeys *up in* the tree"	
sequence	"remember the *last* thing the peddler did" "that was *after* he had thrown his cap"	

Increasing the Power of Instruction

Emphasizing math-related vocabulary

Throughout the readings and the discussions, the teacher frequently uses math-related language (see Table 3.2). As these readings demonstrate, there are many occasions for teachers to incorporate mathematics naturally without shortchanging children's learning in language and literacy; this can be done by sharing mathematical language and concepts during conversation about storybooks (Greenes, Ginsburg, & Balfanz 2004). From ages 2 to 6, children move from intuitive thinking (where understanding is based on concrete objects and their manipulation) to more formal mathematical thinking (where symbols are used to represent and extend concrete experiences). To make this transition, "children need many experiences that call on them to relate their knowledge to the vocabulary and conceptual framework of mathematics—in other words to 'mathematize' what they intuitively grasp" (NAEYC & NCTM 2002, 6).

Teachers can support children's transition from intuitive to more formal and conceptual thinking in mathematics by using math-related terms as they talk with children, provide directions, and support

	Caps for Sale	*The Puddle Pail*
The Second and Third Readings and Discussion		
cardinal number	"only *16* monkeys, not *17*" "*four* monkeys in the tree"	"*18* feathers" "*25* rocks" "these *three* different collections"
counting word sequence	"*one, two, three, four*"	
number comparison	"just *one more* monkey" "*a lot* of monkeys"	
number operations		"we can *add* them to these collections" "we can keep *adding* caps to our collections"
ordinal number	"what will he do *first*" "which monkeys got their caps *first*" "I'm going to put a *second* copy"	
size and quantity	"as *high*"	"*big* brother" "*little* pieces of string" "this *big* one here with the bright colors at its tip" "which of Sol's collections is *bigger*" "which one has *more* items" "when he collected *more* items, he found *more* rocks" "*how many* cookies"
sequence	"do you remember what happened *next*" "do you remember the *last* thing the peddler did" "but that was *after* they saw the peddler" "which monkeys got their caps *next*"	

interactions among children. For example, during cleanup after center time, a teacher can use detailed and math-related, rather than general, verbal support in giving directions: "Please put the basket of markers back on the *top* shelf, *next to* the scissors rack," rather than "Put the basket of markers on the shelf." Similarly, if a child who is cleaning up in the playhouse asks, "Where do these go?" and holds up a cup and saucer, the teacher might suggest that the child "open the doors to the cupboard and look for *other* cups and saucers that are *just like* the *ones* you are holding" rather than answer, "Inside the cupboard."

Similarly, when helping children sit down for story time, a teacher might use math-related terms: "Jason, you are *one* of the *older* and *taller* children. If you stay in the *middle* up *front* here, children *behind* you won't be able to see the book. There's a good spot over there right *next to* Michelle. Please move so that *everyone* can see the book. Thank you." Or during a transition between a whole group activity and outside play, a teacher might announce, "Okay, today, I'm going to send *three* children at a time to their cubbies to get their jackets and sweaters on. Ana, Sam, and Rashid, you may go *first*. Okay, now I'm going to call *three more* children: Jamie, Keisha, and Sarah, you may walk to your cubbies."

The opportunities for math-related talk during a preschool day are numerous because many words used in mathematics can be incorporated into a broad range of learning contexts: "There might not be *enough* apples for *everyone* who wants *more* to have a *second*, but *enough* for those who want *more*

to have *one-half*." . . . "*All* of the *longest* blocks might be *gone* from the shelf, Matt, but there are *enough* of the *shorter* blocks to build a road that is *just as long as* Keisha's." Children might be advised to put on mittens and scarves to go outside, because it is *much* colder today than it was yesterday. Similarly, a teacher might comment as the children put on their mittens, "Mittens have *one big* space for *all four* of our fingers, and then a *second smaller* space for a thumb, don't they?" And to a child who has dropped his marker cap on the floor and can't locate it, a teacher might say, "I see the cap from your marker *under* the table, right *next to* the *front* legs of Maria's chair."

When preschool teachers use more math-related talk throughout the preschool day, children not only pick up the vocabulary, but their mathematical knowledge increases, as well (Klibanoff et al. 2006). As the examples provided here demonstrate, children's general vocabulary development and listening comprehension are also aided when their math-related vocabulary increases, given the wide use of math-related terms in the discussions that teachers and parents have with children during the course of a day.

◆ ◆ ◆

Teachers have many strategies and techniques to use during story time to maximize children's learning in the language, literacy, and mathematical domains, a variety of which we have explored here. In the next chapter, we will focus on a different type of storybook written with a more explicit mathematical intent.

Reflection questions

1. What are the benefits of reading a storybook multiple times?

2. Why is it preferable to use later readings rather than the initial reading to prompt math-related discussions?

3. How did Ms. Freeman extend the learning opportunities presented in *The Puddle Pail* and *Caps for Sale* outside the story reading context? What other activities might you plan to follow up the reading of these books?

4. How can you help children develop skill in inferential thinking?

Increasing the Power of Instruction

4

Using Predictable-Text Books with an Explicit Math Focus

In addition to traditional narratives such as *Inch by Inch*, teachers also read preschool children *predictable-text* books, which use one or more devices to make their text easy for young children to remember. These books are particularly conducive to integrating math, literacy, and language instruction. Many math concepts are orderly and predictable, making them especially suitable for presentation in a predictable-text format. And predictable-text books are easy for children to join in on and are often read during circle time. Before long, children begin to chime in as their teacher reads, just as they join in when singing songs or reciting poems.

The characteristics that make predictable-text books easy for children to remember and comprehend include:

- rhyming words;
- rhythmic sentence structure;
- repetition of a basic *sentence frame*, with only slight variations;
- refrains and other text that repeats from page to page or spread to spread;
- cumulative text (e.g., each page adds a new sentence to the previous text, which is repeated);
- placement of only one idea or thought on each page or spread; and

- closely related illustrations and text (e.g., illustrations depict every item mentioned in the text, illustrations have recurring formats or motifs) (Schickedanz 1999, 77).

A *sentence frame* provides convenient places for varied material to be inserted into an otherwise unchanging structure. For example, the sentences "'Honk, honk' went the little red truck," and "'Beep, beep' went the little green car," have the same sentence structure of "[noise, noise] went the little [color] [vehicle]." Only the inserted content varies. This characteristic and the others mentioned above enable even very young children to read along with adults (Schickedanz 1999).

Reading these kinds of books differs from reading narratives, and the types of discussions that follow storybook readings are often not suitable for predictable-text books. Predictable-text books organized around a math concept, for example, better lend themselves to follow-up activities in small groups or during center time than to reading at circle time. In this chapter, we'll follow our teacher, Ms. Freeman, through three readings of the predictable-text book *One Duck Stuck*, by Phyllis Root. Then we will discuss a few other examples of predictable-text books that offer special features. With additional teacher support, basic mathematical aspects in number concept books can be highlighted and extended to increase children's learning beyond the levels typically attained when children simply listen to a book read aloud. We'll also see how the teacher emphasizes and extends children's language and literacy learning throughout these readings.

This book

In *One Duck Stuck*, a duck whose foot gets stuck in the mud is helped by a series of animals, beginning with two fish and ending with ten dragonflies. But despite the help from nine different groups of animals, the duck remains stuck in the mud until all of the animals work together to free him. The book is organized around the mathematical concept of *one more*, which is important for children's understanding of number.

Even though a preschool child often has a well-developed counting schema—he can recite the number-word sequence and can accurately connect each number word to an item in a group of objects—the child might not be able to answer a question such as "Who would have more trucks, if Matt has four and Luis has six?" In other words, counting skill alone does not lead children to an understanding of quantitative relationships (Baroody 1987; Baroody 2004; Griffin 2004). To build true quantitative knowledge, children must reflect on number relationships. Children build this knowledge by manipulating sets of objects in various ways (e.g., adding items to a set or taking items away, matching items in one set to the items in another, and so on). Exposure to the *one more* concept books can also contribute to this knowledge, especially when teachers use strategies that help children focus explicitly on the *one more* structure.

Two refrains are used throughout *One Duck Stuck* ("Help! Help! Who can help?" and "We can! We can!"), along with two repeating sentence frames into which each new animal's name, its action, and a new description of the marsh (e.g., "swampy, chompy," "pricky, sticky") are inserted. The sound made by the animal featured on each page (e.g., "splish, splish" and "clomp, clomp") is always repeated. These text patterns, along with the use of Arabic numerals and rhyming words in large, bold

type, make the book highly predictable and thus easy for children to learn.

Children typically begin to chime in on the two refrains ("Help! Help! Who can help?" and "We can! We can!") after the teacher has read only a few pages. The second refrain is positioned at the very beginning of the first page of each new two-page spread. Its position almost compels a teacher to turn to the next page immediately after reading, "Help! Help! Who can help?" which is located at the end of the previous page. The teacher also will want to quickly read the rest of the text on each page, given the duck's predicament and the children's interest in knowing whether he will get out of the mud. The children catch on quickly to the refrains, the repeating sentence frames, and the repetition used for the sound description words. The strong predictable structure of the book pulls children into participating.

The first reading

Children benefit from multiple readings of predictable-text books, just as they do from multiple readings of narrative storybooks. However, the techniques and style of reading differ, as we will see here.

Ms. Freeman begins by reading the title and author, underlining them with her finger, and pointing out the duck pictured on the cover. She also says, "Hmmm, one duck *stuck?* Let's read the book and see what happens to this duck." Then she reads the first page, which introduces the duck and his problem. After she reads, "Help! Help! Who can help?" on the second page of the first spread, she turns the page immediately to read, "We can! We can!" Then she points to the large number 2 printed on this page and to the small pictures of the two fish located to the right of this numeral, and reads the beginning of the text as she does so: "Two fish, tails going swish, swim to the duck. Splish, splish."

Because this is a new book for the children, they do not yet know the patterns in the text. They listen attentively to these pages without chiming in. By the time the teacher reaches the point in the story where five frogs appear, the children begin to join in on portions of the text, including the two refrains, the stable parts of the two repeating sentences, and the second of the two repetitions of each sound word. This is what the children's participation sounded like during the teacher's reading of the text:

Ms. Freeman and children: "We can! We can!"

Ms. Freeman turns the page and points first to the large numeral 5 printed to the left of the five frogs, and then quickly to the small pictures of the five frogs just as she begins reading.

Ms. Freeman and children: "Five frogs . . .

Ms. Freeman: " . . . hopping on logs, jump to the duck. Plop . . . "

Ms. Freeman and children: " . . . plop. No luck. The duck stays stuck deep in the muck down by the . . . "

Ms. Freeman: " . . . creaky, croaky . . . "

Ms. Freeman and children: " . . . marsh."

She points to the refrain on the second page of the spread, and as she begins to read the children join in.

Ms. Freeman and children: "Help! Help! Who can help?"

As we can see, the children joined in on quite a lot of the text. In this first reading, Ms. Freeman does not comment much about the story, except to express an occasional concern about the poor duck, and to wonder out loud whether the animals will be able to free him. She also does not provide any explicit support for helping children grasp the book's *one more* structure. Knowing that the children are enjoying the book and are concentrating hard on the patterns in the text that allow them to participate, Ms. Freeman focuses almost entirely on supporting their efforts by simply reading the book without much interruption. She makes sure to vary her pacing and facial expressions at key points to encourage the children to join her aloud.

The very brief discussion following the first reading focuses on the plot and themes of the story—how hard the animals worked, and on how thoughtful they were to help a fellow animal in trouble. Ms. Freeman asks the children whether their feet have ever been stuck in the mud. Although none of the children has been stuck, one child says

that he and his mom were once "stuck in traffic." Another says that her birthday cake once "stuck to the pan," and her grandma had to bake a new one. Ms. Freeman tells the children that her feet have never been stuck in mud either, but that one time her car got stuck in the snow, and a neighbor pushed her car to help get it out of the snowbank. This discussion helps give the story a real-world context, aids the children in visualizing the duck's situation, and provides a variety of contexts in which the meaning of "stuck" can be considered.

The second reading

The next day during circle time, Ms. Freeman reads the book again. This time, she does not read all of the text on each page. Instead, she focuses explicitly on counting the animals with the children and discussing their actions, as the book's format provides an interesting opportunity to count the same number of animals in two different physical arrangements. Recognizing that the same quantity can be represented in multiple ways (e.g., five buttons in a pile versus in a row) is an important math concept for young children to grasp (Copley 2000; NCTM 2000).

On the first page of each new spread there is a large, bold Arabic numeral, followed by small pictures of the new animals that have come to help. The right-hand page shows larger pictures of the animals, which are scattered about on the page performing actions they hope will free the duck. Thus, there are two opportunities on each spread to

Table 4.1

Examples of higher-level words used in teacher commentary

adults	encourage	offered
beak	flipped	review
blossoms	hanging	rope
branch	land	sink
cheering	next to	young
diving	noticed	

count the animals, one in a fairly easy context and the other in a more difficult one. The challenging second page offers the teacher an opportunity to support the development of children's counting skills in a situation where items are not arranged in an orderly fashion. It demonstrates that the physical arrangement of items does not alter their number. The second page also provides opportunities for the teacher to model language: Many descriptive and relational terms can be used to indicate an animal's location, size, and actions. The teacher can also use rich language when responding to children's comments. (For examples of higher-level vocabulary related to the discussion of *One Duck Stuck*, see Table 4.1.)

Ms. Freeman discusses the page that features five frogs. She has already focused on the groups of two, three, and four animals that tried to help the duck. In addition to counting the animals on each page, Ms. Freeman asks questions to prompt children's thinking. The prompts focus on helping the children notice the numbers printed on each page and count the animals. Ms. Freeman also responds to children's comments and questions.

These prompts and conversations are different than those she used when discussing *Caps for Sale* and the other two narratives. They are narrower in focus and do not address issues of plot.

Ms. Freeman: Here are the frogs that offered to help. Here's the number 5 [points to the numeral], because five frogs showed up. Let's count the frogs together.

She points to the small pictures of the frogs on the left-hand page and counts. The children join in.

And all five of the frogs are over here [gestures toward the right-hand page of the spread], trying to help the duck. Let's see if we can find all five of the frogs. I see three frogs jumping up and down. Two are in front of the duck and one is behind it. Do you see them? [She points to them.] And then I see two more, one diving into the water headfirst, the other climbing up on the duck's back.

After describing their locations, she points to all five frogs and leads the children in counting them.

Ms. Freeman and children: 1, 2, 3, 4, 5.

Sam: He's jumping really high.

Ana: There's one on the duck.

Jamie: Hey, that one's jumping upside down.

Ms. Freeman: Oh, do you mean this frog over here, the one with its head in the water? [She points to a frog.]

Jamie: Yes, his head's in the water.

Ms. Freeman: Yes, he seems to have flipped himself over. Or, maybe he was over here on the land [points] and then jumped headfirst into the water. And you are right. This frog is also on this duck. I wonder what this frog is thinking. Why did he think getting on the duck's back would help? [She points to the frog.] Do you think that will help the duck get its foot unstuck?

Ana: He's pushing him, pushing him out of the mud.

Ms. Freeman: Mmmm . . . maybe. He might be trying to push the duck out of the mud, but I'm thinking that actually he's just making the duck heavier. If he's on the duck, it might make the duck's foot sink even deeper into the mud. The other three frogs are over here. See the two here in front of the duck, and this one behind? [She points to these frogs.] I wonder how they are helping?

Sarah: They're jumping.

Ms. Freeman: Yes, they are. Do you think they might be trying to encourage the duck to get out of the mud? They are cheering him on. But did that work?

Sarah: No. He's still stuck.

Jamie: They need more friends to help or it won't work.

Ms. Freeman: Right, it didn't work. He's still stuck. Looks like it is kind of hard to jump when your foot's stuck, isn't it? Let's look at another page and review how other animals tried to help. [She flips ahead to the page in the book with eight possums.] Okay, here are the possums, eight possums. [She points to the numeral 8 printed on the page, and then to the pictures of the possums, as she and the children count them.]

We see the possums over here, too, trying to help the duck. [She points to the right-hand page of the spread.] Let's find all eight possums. 1 . . .

She points to one possum, then looks out to signal the children to join her in searching for and counting the rest.

Ms. Freeman and children: . . . 2, 3, 4, 5, 6, 7, 8.

Keisha: Two baby ones.

Ms. Freeman: Two baby ones? Where are there two babies? Oh, right here [points]. You are right. I hadn't noticed before that there are both big possums and little possums. These three [points] look a little smaller than the others, don't they?

Keisha: They're babies.

Ms. Freeman: They sure look like babies, don't they?

Keisha: And they're on their mother over there [she points to the opposite page].

Ms. Freeman: Oh, I see what you mean. Two babies are on their mother's back, and this little possum is holding onto his mother's tail. I hope he doesn't let go and fall!

Rashid: That one's got his tail.

Ms. Freeman: Oh, yes. And look! Does everyone see this possum over here [points]? He's also hanging upside down. So, let's see whether there are eight possums altogether on these pages. 1 . . . [children join in counting] . . . 2, 3, 4, 5, 6, 7, 8. Yes, there are eight possums: five adults, 1, 2, 3, 4, 5 [points as she counts them again], and three young ones, babies, 1, 2, 3 [points].

What idea did the possums have for helping the duck? What did they make with the flowers, the blossoms?

Rashid: A rope.

Ms. Freeman: Yes, they made a rope out of flowers. It looks like the duck is trying to hold onto the flower rope with its beak. I wonder what might happen to the flower rope if the duck pulls really hard on it.

Sam: He'll take it.

Rashid: It will break.

Ms. Freeman: Yes, the flower rope would break pretty easily, if the duck pulled on it.

The teacher continues with this approach as she and the children review all of the remaining pages.

The third reading

Later in the week the teacher reads the book a third time. As the children now have a good grasp of the book's plot and structure, Ms. Freeman turns the page quickly after the children shout the refrain "We can! We can!" and she points to the large numeral printed on the left page of each new spread. She mouths the number but remains silent as the children read it aloud. Then she continues reading the rest of the text on each spread. She reads the whole book in this way (which the children thoroughly enjoy, given their familiarity with the story). Then Ms. Freeman turns back to the page where the two fish are featured and begins to focus specifically on the *one more* number concept around which the book is organized.

Ms. Freeman: Let's go through the pages again and try to remember or figure out how many animals come to help each time. Okay, here are the two fish that were the first animals that tried to help the duck. On the next page some moose come to help. How many moose? 1, 2 . . .

She points to the numeral 3 on the left page, and then starts to recite the counting word sequence, pausing to scaffold children's recall of the next number.

Children: 3!

Ms. Freeman: Yes, [turns the page to show the moose] three moose come. The number three comes right after the number two. Three is just one more than two. Next, some crickets come to help. How many crickets? 1, 2, 3 . . .

Children: 4!

Ms. Freeman: That's right, four crickets arrive [turns the page]. The number four comes right after three. Four is just one more than three. Next, some frogs come. How many frogs? 1, 2, 3, 4 . . .

She continues in this way through the rest of the book.

In this additional review after the third reading of the book, Ms. Freeman did not read all of the text again. Instead, she focused on the number of animals that arrived each time, stressing that the new number of animals was just *one more* than the number of animals in the previous group. Her strategy was to name the type of animal that came next and ask children how many of that animal showed up. In this way, the children could focus squarely on the relationship between two successive numbers in the standard counting sequence.

Ms. Freeman used a thoughtful plan to guide the three readings of this book, designed first to engage children with the book and to encourage their participation; then to increase their awareness of the number of each kind of animal (and that different arrangements of the same objects do not alter their number); and finally to bring children's attention more fully to the *one more* relationship between consecutive numbers in the counting sequence. She also used rich language in discussing the book with the children; prompted them to think about the animals' locations, thoughts, physical characteristics, and the effects of their actions; and tried hard to understand children's comments and questions.

In her second and third readings in particular, she also engaged in a good deal of "math talk" with the children, who in turn used math talk in their own comments. Of course, *One Duck Stuck* is a predictable-text book organized around a math concept, which tends to lead to a fairly high level of math talk. (See Table 4.2 for examples of Ms. Freeman's and the children's math-related vocabulary from the second reading.)

The teacher also supported children's literacy skills by underlining with her finger some of the print as she read it, and by modeling the left-to-right order in which the pages of a book are read. Rather than attempt too much in any one reading, Ms. Freeman thoughtfully used each of the three readings to focus on different things.

Follow-up activities

After the third reading, Ms. Freeman places the book in the classroom library for children's independent use during center time. Ms. Freeman also makes available felt pieces for use on a flannel board, if children wish to retell the story in that way. Preparing the follow-up activities, she traced and cut out a felt piece of each animal. Then she glued together each animal group on a strip of felt, and placed the Arabic numeral indicating their quantity to the far left. This design helps the children to organize the pieces in order to retell the story, while minimizing clutter in the flannel board area.

Ms. Freeman also prepared a matching game, consisting of one small picture of each type of animal that came to help the duck. She glued these pictures in a column on the left side of a piece of poster board. She drew a line to the right of each of the nine animals pictured. She also made a set of nine cards—one each for the nine sound words

Table 4.2

Examples of math-related words used in the second reading of *One Duck Stuck*

Below are examples of math-related words and phrases that a teacher and the children in her class might use in their discussion of this book. Please note that many of these words are not used in the book itself, but are incorporated into the story reading context to enhance children's mathematics learning.

Teacher's Math Talk	
cardinal number	"because *five* frogs showed up" "all *five* of the frogs are over here" "I see *three* of the frogs jumping up and down" "okay, here are the possums, *eight* possums"
spatial location	"jumped *out into* the water, *headfirst*" "see the two here *in front of* the duck, and this one *behind*"
number comparison	"then I see two *more*" "try to remember *how many* animals come each time" "three is just *one more* than two" "*how many* frogs came"
size and quantity	"he's just making the duck *heavier*" "it might make the duck's foot sink even *deeper*" "I hadn't noticed before that there are *big* possums and *little* possums"
counting word sequence	"let's find all eight possums, *1, 2, 3, 4, 5, 6, 7, 8*" "five adults, *1, 2, 3, 4, 5*"
sequence	"four comes *right after* three"
numeral recognition	"here's the number *5*"

Children's Math Talk	
cardinal number	"there's *one* on the duck" "*two* baby ones" "here are the *eight* possums"
spatial location	"he's pushing him, pushing him *out of* the mud" "hey, that one's jumping *upside down*" "his head's *in* the water" "and they're *on* their mother *over there*"
number comparison	"they need *more* friends to help or it won't work"
size and quantity	"he's jumping really *high*"

from the book (*splish, clomp, pleep, plop, plunk, sloosh, slosh, slink, zing*). Ms. Freeman laminated the poster board and the word cards, and then placed a small piece of self-adhesive fabric on the middle of each line and on the back of each word card, making it easy for the children to match a sound with its corresponding animal.

Ms. Freeman introduces these matching materials during whole group time the day after the third reading of *One Duck Stuck*. She clips the poster board with the pictures of each animal onto a chart stand and then reviews the list with the children, one animal at a time, helping them recall the sound each group of animals made as they helped the duck. Starting with the picture of the fish, she helps children recall that *splish* was the sound on the fish page. Next, she speaks the word carefully, segmenting its initial phonemes. She reminds the children that the letter *s* is used to write the sound /s/. Then she asks what letter is used to write the sound /p/.

After isolating the beginning phoneme(s) for each of the nine words and linking these to letters used to write the sounds, Ms. Freeman leads the children in finding the word card that matches the animal's picture. For example, after determining with the children that the letters *s* and *p* are needed to write the first two sounds of *splish*, Ms. Freeman says, "Okay, we need to find the word that starts with *s* and then has *p* next." She writes these two letters together on the board to help children keep them firmly in their minds; then she shows the word cards to the children one by one until they find the correct one. They encounter the *sloosh* card before *splish*, which provides an opportunity for the teacher to compare the sounds /s/ /l/ with /s/ /p/, and to remind children that to read a word they must look at more than its first letter. This idea is further emphasized as they encounter the words *pleep, plop, sloosh, slosh,* and *slink*.

The teacher's approach helps children to develop phoneme segmentation skills and to further consolidate their letter recognition and their knowledge of letter-sound associations. After using these materials in a whole group session,

Ms. Freeman puts them and a copy of the book out for the children's independent use during center time. During the three weeks that they are available, many children use the materials. Ms. Freeman stops by to observe and assist in their use, as needed. After the matching materials have been removed, Ms. Freeman notices children pointing to these sound words in the book itself, which remains in the classroom library for many weeks.

Highlighting special features of predictable-text books

Sometimes a predictable-text book has special characteristics, such as a unique style of illustration or an additional *text track* (i.e., two different, but related, sets of information being conveyed to the reader). In such cases, teachers may want to adapt their instruction to take advantage of these features.

Facilitating children's comprehension of books with multiple text tracks

An example of a predictable-text book with a special text feature is Lois Ehlert's *Fish Eyes: A Book You Can Count On*. This colorful book, written in verse, relates an imaginary journey that introduces a variety of fish in progressively larger groups, from one to ten. Each new group has a unique physical feature (such as spots or stripes) or action (such as jumping or darting). We learn from the first few introductory pages that someone human is imagining that he or she were a fish. The remainder of the book shows this imaginary fish traveling through rivers and seas.

The text on the majority of the book's pages is simple and brief, but *Fish Eyes* has a special feature—two parallel text tracks. The main text, printed prominently in very large type, follows the sentence frame of "[numeral] [number word] [descriptor] fish"—for example, "2 two jumping fish" and "9 nine flashy fish." The secondary text is printed in much smaller type next to a little, green fish at the edge of each page. This secondary text prompts the children to think about what comes next—for example, "9 nine flashy fish plus me makes 10"—and follows the sentence frame of "[numeral] [number word] [descriptor] fish plus me makes [numeral]."

Ms. Freeman's first reading of *Fish Eyes* focuses on number concepts (i.e., the number of fish pictured in each group). Other vocabulary and content will be highlighted in subsequent readings, rather than in the first, to avoid interfering with the children's understanding of the book's main focus. (As a follow-up to a third reading, for example, a focus on the descriptive words will help develop children's vocabulary and their knowledge of fish and other animals. However, introducing such vocabulary too soon would undermine children's comprehension of the number concepts so central to the book.)

Because she thinks the secondary text track will make more sense to the children *after* they have a grasp of the book's basic structure, Ms. Freeman waits until the second reading to introduce the little, green fish. Then, during the second reading, which immediately follows the first, she makes the most of this feature, focusing almost exclusively on it. The little, green fish and its statements concerning addition (e.g., "1 one green fish plus me makes 2") are difficult to see against the dark background of the book's pages. But by letting the children become familiar with the flow of the book first, Ms. Freeman increases the attention they can give to the feature and the explicit instructional support she provides for the concept of *one more.*

It's unusual for a book to have a second set of text like this. To facilitate the children's understanding, she takes some time to explain what is happening.

Ms. Freeman: I want to show you something now that I didn't show you when I read the book the first time. Down here in the corner [points to the little, green fish] we see a little fish. This is the little fish that a human is imagining himself to be.

Here [points to the black text near the fish], it says "Follow me." The little fish says this to invite us to look at everything that he sees in his mind as he imagines himself swimming in rivers and the sea. The pages are so dark that you can just barely see the little, green fish and the words that are printed near him in black. I'll show the book to you, up close.

She holds the book closer to the children, moving it from side to side in front of the group to give everyone a chance to locate the fish and the words, which are quite difficult to see against the dark blue page.

Ms. Freeman: When I read this book the first time, I didn't read the part that the little fish says. This time, I'm going to read *just* that part. But before I start, I am going to put some things up on our flannel board. I have a felt hand with its fingers and thumb held up, and another felt hand with its fingers and thumb folded down against its palm [places the two hands on the flannel board]. We'll use these hands later on in the story.

I'm going to start right here on this page [points to the page] where the little fish says, "Follow me." I'll turn the page so we can follow the little fish—who is actually the person *pretending* to be a fish—on his imaginary journey.

Here we see one big, green fish that the little fish saw, and then, down here, the little fish says, "1 one green fish plus me makes 2." The little fish is adding himself to the one green fish he saw, and he's saying that this makes two fish. He's right, isn't he? If we have one of something [raises one of her own fingers] and we add one more of something to it [raises a second finger], we have two of something.

She turns the page. Several children voice agreement and some use their fingers to confirm the addition.

Ms. Freeman: On this page, after the little fish sees two jumping fish, he says, "2 two jumping fish plus me makes 3." He's right, isn't he?

Children: Yes.

Ms. Freeman: Yes, because if we start with two of something [raises two fingers] and add one more to them [raises a third finger], we have three of something, don't we? Okay, I'm going to turn the page.

Ana: Three fish!

Ms. Freeman: Yes, the little fish sees three smiling fish, and says, "3 three smiling fish plus me makes 4." [She holds up four fingers, then turns the page.] Then, the little fish sees "4 four striped fish . . . " [She underlines the text at the top of the page with her finger, then continues reading.] "4 four striped fish plus me makes 5." [She holds up her fingers as before.] And then [turns the page], the little fish sees five spotted fish and says, "5 five spotted fish plus me makes 6."

At this point, she explains that she has run out of fingers to keep track of the total number of fish, as her other hand is holding the book. She refers to the felt hands on the flannel board, and explains how these will help.

Ms. Freeman: We can pretend that each finger here [points to the first felt hand, with all fingers raised] is counting a fish. We just read that the little fish said, "5 five spotted fish plus me makes 6," so this hand [points to the first hand again] has five fingers for the five spotted fish.

I'm going to raise one finger on this *second* felt hand to add the little, green fish to the five spotted fish that he just imagined that he saw. [She pulls up one finger on the second flannel hand.] Five fish [points toward the first hand] and one more fish [points to the single finger raised on the second hand] makes six fish altogether. 1, 2 . . .

Ms. Freeman and children: 3, 4, 5, 6.

Ms. Freeman: Let's keep going [turns the page]. Next, the little fish saw "6 six fantailed fish" [underlines the text as she reads]. He said, "6 six fantailed fish . . . " [pauses for the children to chime in on the next three words, which are now very familiar] "plus me makes . . . 7." I'll add another finger to

this hand, to show our seventh fish [pulls one more finger up on the second felt hand].

Ms. Freeman continues in a similar fashion through "9 nine flashy fish plus me makes 10." She reads the two pages that follow ("Then, I'd keep swimming until I would see all of those fish eyes looking at me"), then counts the 22 colorful eyes pictured, inviting the children to count along. On the last page, she reads, "Good-bye! Hope to see you again."

Now that the children have been introduced to the little, green fish and understand his purpose, Ms. Freeman feels comfortable combining both text tracks together in her third reading of the book. During this third reading, which takes place a few days later, she reads the bold main text (underlining it with her finger), counts the fish pictured, and reads about the little fish adding himself to the group.

This time, Ms. Freeman does not use the felt hands and fingers. Instead, she reads the text at the top of each page and then reads the secondary text in which the little fish adds himself to each group. She quickly counts, the fish on the page while pointing to each one. After this, she pauses very briefly before counting one more to mark the addition of the little fish. As she counts, she points to each corresponding fish, and the children count with her.

In this way, she uses pacing and emphasis to mark the total number of fish in the initial group, the addition of the little fish, and the resulting sum. The reading of each page works well with this approach, and it models a strategy for young children to use in determining the sum when adding one more item to a group.

Facilitating children's comprehension of illustrations

Ten Black Dots, a rhyming predictable-text book by Donald Crews, focuses on counting from one to ten. *Ten Black Dots* has a unique illustration feature: Most numbers are shown in two different pictures depicting two different arrangements of black dots, one on the left page and one on the right. For

One of the typical two-page spreads from *Ten Black Dots.*

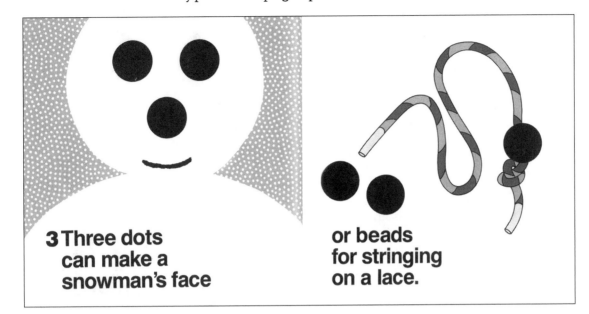

3 Three dots can make a snowman's face

or beads for stringing on a lace.

example, on the spread for the number three, the black dots on one page form a snowman's two eyes and mouth, while the black dots on the opposite page form the three beads of a necklace.

This design reinforces a concept mentioned earlier in this chapter—that the same number of items (dots, in this case) can be arranged differently, and that arrangement does not affect quantity. Representations help make mathematical ideas concrete and encourage reflection (NCTM 2000). When children grasp that they can represent the same quantity in different ways, they begin to use the process of representation on their own to make sense of math problems and concepts.

Several times, however, *Ten Black Dots* departs from the basic two-page spread format described above. In one departure, we see six dots, representing marbles, arranged in two sets of three. Each set is held in the palm of a hand. Similarly, eight dots represent the wheels of a train. Four wheels are attached to the train engine on one page; the second group of four is on a train car on the opposite page. Later, two unique sets of nine black dots and two unique sets of ten black dots are used for different things, and are displayed on different spreads. The nine black dots used as toy soldiers'

heads take up one full spread, and the nine black dots that are pennies in a piggybank take up a second full spread. On the next spread, we see ten black dots, representing balloons stuck in trees. On the following spread, the ten black dot "balloons" float freely toward the sky.

Teachers can increase children's learning when they highlight and explain illustrations such as those in *Ten Black Dots*. For example, on the spread exploring groups of two—where the black dots first depict the eyes of a fox, then the holes in two keys—Ms. Freeman comments, "Animals and people have two eyes. Keys don't have eyes to see with, like ours. But they do have little holes in the middle, which could make us think of eyes." And on the page with five dots used as buttons on one page, and five dots representing portholes on the other, Ms. Freeman counts both sets of five dots and then explains that portholes are the windows on a boat. She continues through the book in this way, counting dots and encouraging children to help by reciting the number words with her, then explaining some of the objects that are depicted in the illustrations. In doing so, she helps children understand that a group of items can be rearranged without changing its quantity, and she helps children learn the meanings of many words.

Just as with the other books, Ms. Freeman reads this book multiple times. After the second reading, she introduces a follow-up activity. She shows the children several pictures, each of which incorporates round black dots in a manner similar to the illustrations in *Ten Black Dots*. For example, in a picture of two trees, eight black dots are used to represent eight apples. Eight black dots are also used for the eyes of four honeybees. Ms. Freeman pairs the pictures with accompanying rhyming verses that she has composed: "Eight black dots are apples on trees, and also the eyes of four hungry bees." For the pictures featuring four dots, the verse reads, "Four black balls are rolling down the hill, or all lined up on a windowsill." She tells the children that she will show them more pictures during small group time the next day, and that they can help think of rhyming verses to go along with them.

As the children grow more familiar with the book, they increasingly chime in during readings. By the time Ms. Freeman reads the book a third time (two days after the second reading), the children participate a great deal. For the discussion following this reading, she shares the concept book *What Do Wheels Do All Day?* In this book by April Jones Prince and Giles Laroche, wheels are shown on many things (e.g., a wheelbarrow, wagon, bicycle, wheelchair, scooter, stroller, and so on). Ms. Freeman focuses the discussion on the number of wheels on each item shown and the page in *Ten Black Dots* where the item could have been featured. Because wheels are round, it is easy for children to make the connection between the illustrations of wheels and the illustrations of dots in *Ten Black Dots*.

At the end of this discussion, Ms. Freeman says she can imagine a number book where each page features one more wheel instead of one more dot:

> For example, a wheelbarrow could go on the page for number one; a wheelbarrow and a pinwheel could go on the page for number two; a bicycle and a pinwheel could go on the page for number three. . . .

Ms. Freeman makes the book available during small group time for a few days. She suggests that the children use it along with the pictures she drew and showed to them the previous day, and that they think about what kind of number book they might like to make.

Ms. Freeman used the discussions following the readings of *Ten Black Dots* to extend children's learning in several ways. For example, she shared verses she wrote that were modeled after the verses written by the author of *Ten Black Dots*. By doing this, she highlighted the book's structure in a very explicit way, which helped children understand it. Beyond this, she indicated to children that she and they could be writers, too. Used in conjunction with *Ten Black Dots*, the book *What Do Wheels Do All Day?* helped the children think like authors and illustrators. It also provided the basis for children to think about making books of their own during small group time.

◆ ◆ ◆

In using these predictable-text books—all of which dealt overtly with mathematical concepts—the teacher integrated instruction in language, literacy, and mathematics. The oral language support Ms. Freeman provided aided children's comprehension of the illustrations and vocabulary, while also supporting the children's understanding of math concepts. She also integrated literacy concepts—such as main characters and the function of information and concept books—into the total experience. Finally, she reinforced print concepts, such as left-to-right progression.

Having now looked in these first four chapters at integration across the domains, we next turn our attention to integration across the various learning contexts—beginning in Chapter 5 with circle time.

Reflection questions

1. How do the features of predictable-text books compensate for preschool children's limited prior knowledge and thus support their conceptual and literacy learning?

2. In what ways do predictable-text reading techniques differ from narrative reading techniques? Which techniques are the same?

3. How did the follow-up activities to the readings of *One Duck Stuck* and *Ten Black Dots* support the integration of language, literacy, and mathematics? What types of activities would you plan for your own classroom?

4. How did Ms. Freeman extend the mathematics themes introduced in the books into both center time and small group contexts? Why? How did her use of these two contexts differ?

II Integration Across Learning Contexts

5

Integration in Whole Group/Circle Time

Circle time is an important whole group, teacher-guided learning context. As discussed in the introduction, a balance in the daily preschool schedule between choice periods and teacher-guided group experiences can provide a full range of opportunities to address all aspects of children's learning (Bowman, Donavan, & Burns 2001; Dickinson 2001; Senechal & LeFevre 2002; Justice et al. 2003; Dickinson & Porche 2005).

Many large group activities provide enjoyable and educational experiences for the group as a whole, such as singing and reciting poems together. Other large group activities also enrich each child's experience, but in a somewhat different way. Consider a short group discussion about a recent field trip to the zoo. Each child's comments about his or her favorite animals prompt reflections from other children. The teacher's guidance and support enable children to engage in an extended and coherent discussion of the experience. Planning a whole group zoo discussion as a follow-up to the field trip extends the learning experience more than does simply encouraging spontaneous conversation with friends about the zoo by placing model animals in the block area or information books about zoo animals in the library area.

Of course, teachers will engage with children on an individual basis throughout the day, outside of whole group time. Such individual engagement, however, requires considerable time. Given the number of children in a class compared with the number of teachers, it's difficult to find the time each day for meaningful engagement with each child or even small groups of children. Moreover, at some times, teacher engagement may interrupt children's focus. For example, when children are engaged in play with toy animals in the block area, asking, "What did you like best about our trip to the zoo?" can disrupt their dramatic play. Both teacher-initiated and child-initiated activities have specific dynamics and contribute uniquely to children's social and cognitive development.

Certain kinds of learning also require some explicit explanations and instruction. Learning about rhyming words, words that begin with the same sounds, and the number word sequence used in counting are three such kinds of learning. Teacher-guided experiences that introduce children to these topics should be provided in a variety of settings, including large groups, helping to ensure that all children in the class have access to a base amount of instruction, especially on key points. Such guidance can be given during circle time.

In some preschools, there is more than one circle time each day—morning meeting and a general circle time later in the day. Morning meeting is a specific kind of circle time in which teachers typically lead children in singing a "Good Morning" song, engage them in routines involving attendance and classroom jobs, and orient them to the activities of the day. In more general circle time, the class may sing songs, share poems, listen to predictable-text books (though this may be a separate part of the day's schedule), and play math, language, and literacy games.

Scheduling two distinct and relatively short circle times in different parts of the preschool day—each lasting about 20 to 25 minutes—is more appropriate than one longer period lasting about 45 minutes. When whole group sessions run too long, they tax preschool children's capacity to sit, engage, and attend to the information being presented. In this chapter, we will focus only on the general type of circle time, rather than the morning meeting, because it is the more common form in preschool programs.

Some effects of whole group time on children's learning

Although little research has focused on the effects of whole group time on preschool children's learning, a few studies do provide information about features that can make circle time productive for children. In one study of several preschools' large group times throughout the day (story time, circle time, and so on), children's language learning outcomes were higher when the "teacher talk" was more informative and less focused on prohibitions, reprimands, and directions for appropriate behavior (McCartney 1984). In a second study, by Dickinson (2001), informative and challenging talk in preschool was again related to better language learning outcomes. Dickinson identified additional characteristics as predictors of better kindergarten outcomes. In the whole group setting, the predictors are:

- a well-organized large group time with planned activities and prepared materials;

- cognitively challenging teacher talk, such as content-rich explanations and thoughtful questions;
- use of higher-level vocabulary by teachers; and
- avoidance by teachers of lengthy conversations with just one child (which risk losing the attention of the other children).

A third study observed preschool teachers' "math talk" during circle time over a preschool year. The researchers noted the use of nine types of math talk related to number sense and operations (Klibanoff et al. 2006). They found that teachers used math-related vocabulary during instruction that was planned specifically to have a math focus, as well as incidentally in instruction with other focuses during circle time. They also found wide variations in the number of different kinds and the overall amount of math talk used by different teachers. For example, teachers' math talk ranged from a low of one math-related word to a high of 104 math-related words within a single observation of circle time across the 26 teachers included in the study. The researchers found a strong relationship between the number of instances in which teachers used math-related vocabulary during circle time and the growth over the year in children's math skills and understanding (Klibanoff et al. 2006).

Planning for circle time

When planning for circle time, teachers should prepare for a few weeks at a time, making sure that a range of beneficial activities are included within this time span. If programming is organized around thematic units, teachers should plan circle time activities for each unit. Each unit typically lasts from two to five weeks depending on the theme's scope.

In planning for each day's circle time, teachers consider how activities vary in terms of goals and duration, and in the behavior they require of children. For example, singing a song or reciting a poem usually takes a fairly short amount of time, and all children and the teacher participate together. Although learning specific words or physical actions associated with a song or poem requires cognitive effort, the instruction is provided by the teacher, and the children receive substantial guidance. In addition, many songs and poems are accompanied by gestures or small actions (e.g., "Clap Our Hands" and "Wheels on the Bus") and large motor movements (e.g., "Head, Shoulders, Knees, and Toes" and "Looby Loo"), or are illustrated with materials the teacher provides. These visual demonstrations increase children's attention, support their learning of verses, and prompt recall. Although new songs, poems, and verses are introduced from time to time, many of the same songs, poems, and finger plays are repeated across days and weeks. Repetition, physical and visual support, and the guidance and participation of the teacher all help children to learn many songs and poems very well, and to participate with comfort and ease when performing them.

Some whole group math activities and verbal clue games are also repeated many times within the preschool year, using similar materials and procedures but with significant variations in detail. Compared with songs and poems, such games require more cognitive effort. For example, with verbal math problems, the framework becomes familiar over time, but each problem contains somewhat different content. (For an example of a verbal math problem activity, see Box 5.1 on the next page.) Solving the problem by acting it out as a story means that a verbal math problem may take more time to complete than does singing a song or reciting a poem. With such activities, children must listen to the scenarios presented and think about them to solve the problems. (See Box 5.2 later in this chapter for an example of a game that can cover a variety of literacy, language, and math topics.)

Many literacy skills activities also use familiar frames, with the specific content changing each time the activity is used. For example, children may be asked to think of words that rhyme with two target words (e.g., "What rhymes with *boat* and *goat*?"). After providing some examples of words that rhyme and modeling the segmentation of their *onsets* from their identical *rime* portions (e.g., *b-oat*, *g-oat*), children are asked to suggest a few words. (The onset portion of a syllable is the initial consonant sound; the rime portion of a syllable is everything

from the vowel to the end of the syllable.) Even though children become familiar with the activity, they must listen, act, and think anew each time they play it with new target words.

Children's development of phonological awareness depends on their access to specific experiences in which adults focus on relevant skills (Senechal & LeFevre 2002; Justice et al. 2003). Children need extensive, explicit, and systematic exposure to rhyming words and words beginning with the same sounds, and they need many opportunities to judge words as similar or different. In addition to exposure and clear examples from the teacher, children need opportunities to generate examples themselves—whether correct or not—and to receive constructive feedback. For example, when a teacher asks, "What rhymes with *cake*?" and a child replies, "Frosting!" a helpful reply might be,

> Well, we do put frosting on a cake. But we are trying to think of words that rhyme with cake. *Cake* and *rake* rhyme. Hear the *ake* in both words? *C-ake, r-ake*? With words that rhyme, the last parts of the words sound alike . . . like *c-ake* and *r-ake*. I wonder what other words rhyme with *cake* and *rake*?

Devoting a small amount of large group time several days a week to activities such as this helps to ensure that all children get the benefit of teacher-guided experience, even though individual follow-up cannot be as thorough or as extended in large groups as it can be in small groups (see Chapter 6).

Predictable-text books, discussed in Chapter 4, are often read in a large group setting. As we've seen, they involve yet another kind of participation. Children listen as the teacher reads the book aloud, and they participate in various ways that differ with each book. Reading a predictable-text book typically takes much longer than singing a song, reciting a poem, or engaging in a literacy skills task. Sometimes, just one reading of a predictable-text book requires almost all of the time allocated for the day's circle. For this reason, the teacher does not read a predictable-text book to children each day. Whether or not a teacher includes such a book during circle time will affect planning, not only for that session but also for circle time sessions on

Box 5.1

How many cars did Keisha have left? A verbal math problem

The teacher tells the story

Ms. Freeman presents the following story problem, which uses the names of two of the children in the class, Keisha and Jamie, and Mrs. Sandish, the class's other teacher:

Ms: Freeman: One day, Keisha was playing in the block area by herself, building a long, wide road out of blocks. When she was done, she took a bunch of little cars out and put them on her road. She wondered how many there were. She counted them: "1, 2, 3, 4, 5, 6," and found out that there were six. It was fun having so many cars to play with.

Keisha moved her cars up and down her road, and sometimes down a ramp to fill them up with gas. She pretended that people were riding in all of the cars, and that they were going shopping, or going to the park, or going to visit their friends.

Keisha was having a very good time playing with the six cars all by herself. Then Jamie came to the block area. He wanted some cars, too. Keisha said, "No, I need them all. I'm playing with them. You can't have any." But Jamie said, "Well, I want some, too. It's not fair for you to have them all." Keisha said, "But I had them first, and I need them all."

Mrs. Sandish heard the children, and went to the block area. She said, "Keisha, we need to share the cars. There are a lot of cars, six cars, and you can't have all of them when a friend wants to play, too."

Keisha said, "Okay," and gave one car to Jamie. Then, Mrs. Sandish said, "And remember, we need to share fairly. You still have a lot of cars, and Jamie has just one. I'm going to ask you to share the cars in a fair way. Make sure that both of you have exactly the same number of cars."

"Okay," Keisha said. She wanted to have a lot of cars, but she knew she had to divide them in a fair way. She and Jamie had to end up with the same number of cars. So she divided her six cars fairly. She also invited Jamie to play with his cars on her road. A big road was something that was easy to share.

She and Jamie had fun playing together with their cars.

Now, here's the question: How many cars did Keisha and Jamie each have, after Keisha shared the cars? Remember, she shared the cars fairly. They both ended up with the same number of cars. I'll remind you that Keisha had six cars to herself before she shared them.

Keisha, how many cars do you think you and Jamie would each have?

The children act out the story

In response to Ms. Freeman's question, Keisha says "four" but quickly revises her answer to "three." Although three is correct, Ms. Freeman wants the children to act out the problem to ensure that everyone understands the solution. After hearing Keisha's thoughts about how many cars she and Jamie would end up with, Ms. Freeman suggests that Keisha and Jamie act out a simplified version of the scenario.

The teacher provides just a few blocks, enough to make a short road, and comments to everyone that Keisha's road was much bigger in the story. She gives six cars to Keisha, and tells her to build a road for the cars while she retells the first part of the story. Then Jamie and Keisha reenact the story, and Mrs. Sandish joins in, too. Ms. Freeman tells the other children that they are the audience. As she rereads the story events, they watch and listen. She encourages their engagement in watching with a few side comments (e.g., "Okay, it's going to take Keisha just a few minutes to divide her cars. We can watch her do that").

Keisha has a few minutes to divide the cars between herself and Jamie when Ms. Freeman reaches that part of the story, and the strategy for dividing is left up to Keisha. She puts all of the cars in a pile next to her, and gives one car to herself and one to Jamie, then another car to herself and another to Jamie, and finally one more car to herself and the last car to Jamie. Keisha is able to divide them equally.

subsequent days, which must incorporate second and third readings of the book.

For each day's circle time, the teacher selects a variety of activities and carefully considers how to sequence them to meet the varied needs of the children in the group and to keep all children interested and engaged. For example, teachers often alternate among the following:

- stand-up and sit-down activities;
- activities that involve actions and speaking and those that require only listening and speaking;
- activities that require turn-taking and those that do not;
- familiar activities and those that are less familiar or completely new; and
- activities that differ in the type and degree of challenges they pose for children's thinking.

In the examples of typical group activities that follow, the focus is on increasing the instructional power of circle time. Several activities are discussed later on in greater detail, illustrating how instruction can be implemented at three different levels—basic, enriched, and highly enriched—over a period of time.

Changing the level of implementation over time increases children's exposure to new vocabulary; it also increases the possibilities for integrating learning from more than one domain. Such gradual increases ensure that children are not overwhelmed with the complexity of an activity when it is first introduced. For example, an emphasis on print and literacy skills can be added later on to an experience that, in its introductory form, focuses only on oral language development. An enriched form of an activity might also use diagrams or charts in ways that not only increase children's general vocabulary but also introduce specific math-related vocabulary.

When an enriched or a highly enriched version of an activity is introduced, the teacher provides extra commentary to support children's transitions into and out of the activity. In other words, when a teacher introduces changes to a basic activity, he or she must then be sure to explain and demonstrate how the activity will work given those changes.

In addition to introducing new vocabulary to the children, these explanations can also expose children to complex language structure in a context where it has considerable physical support and children have some prior knowledge (Weizman & Snow 2001).

A day in circle time

Each day's circle time includes a variety of activities. In our example of one day's circle time, we'll examine the following activities that Ms. Freeman has planned for her classroom:

1. "The More We Get Together"—song, 1–2 minutes
2. "Good-Morning" (Sipe)—poem, 3–4 minutes
3. "Head, Shoulders, Knees, and Toes"—song, 3–4 minutes
4. "BINGO"—song, 3–4 minutes
5. *The Doorbell Rang* (Hutchins)—predictable-text book featuring a math concept, 5–6 minutes

Getting started

The children gather on the rug for circle time. One teacher in the class helps children finish cleaning up after center time, which precedes circle time in this classroom's daily schedule. The second teacher, Ms. Freeman, is already seated at the front of the circle area with materials for the day's activities close at hand. She encourages the children to get seated and talks with them as they gather in front of her. When most of the children have settled down, she begins. Below, we see how this day's circle time proceeds.

1. The first activity—song

Ms. Freeman: Okay, we'll start circle time today with a song you know really well. It's "The More We Get Together." [She starts singing.] "The more we get together, together, together, the more we get together, the happier we'll be. . . . "

The children join in. By the time the song ends, the last child has finished cleaning up and joins the group.

> I saw a lot of happy faces during center time when you were playing with one another. There were a few unhappy times, but we were able to solve those problems.

Box 5.2

Word clues game

In this circle time game, the teacher reinforces vocabulary related to a variety of content domains. If needed, however, this game could focus only on reinforcing math-related terms, such as shapes or numbers. In this way, the game could serve as a follow-up to math-related activities.

How to play

This game can be played during circle time a couple of times per week. The teacher chooses three to five words for children to guess during each game session. Children should have some prior experience with these words, ideally in several different contexts (e.g., through dramatic play, reading, and observation).

The children guess the words based on a variety of verbal clues and visual aids provided by the teacher. The first clue should give appropriate category information. For example, if the word is *rabbit*, the teacher might use "animal" or "mammal" as the category clue (e.g., "This is a mammal"). The next clue should provide some specific information about the particular word ("This animal is covered with fur, and it has long ears").

The teacher should give only two clues before letting children guess. If the children do not guess the item from the first two clues, the teacher can provide another. For the rabbit, the third clue might provide information about its behavior ("This animal likes to eat carrots and lettuce, and it hops instead of runs"). After each word has been guessed, the teacher quickly reviews any visual aids used, noting features that were included in the clues.

When children's guesses are incorrect (as is often the case after the first two clues), the correct parts of their reasoning should be acknowledged, and then another clue should be given. For example, if the children guess "cat," the teacher might say, "I see what you are thinking. A cat is a small, furry animal, but its ears are short, not long, so that's not the animal I'm thinking of." Children's incorrect guesses provide wonderful opportunities

for teachers to add more information and to help children make subtle distinctions. Only saying, "No, that's not what I'm thinking" in response to an incorrect answer does not provide information about why the guess is wrong, nor does it acknowledge what is correct about the child's guess. As Johnson (2004) discusses, it is important for children's learning and social-emotional well-being to acknowledge what is partially correct in their responses and to link this to fuller or more accurate information.

Preparation

Teachers can assemble a list of clues for each word in advance. The teacher also needs a picture or object representing each word, to be shown to the children after the word has been guessed. Pictures and diagrams help us understand meaning; they also help children recall experiences and learn about how things are represented visually. Showing a picture or a diagram after a word has been guessed also helps ensure that children who did not guess the word understand its meaning. If children do not know what a word means, they can't create a visual image of it in their minds. Showing a picture of the object helps children link the word to its meaning.

Time

It usually takes about five or six minutes for children to consider the clues for three to five words. The length of the game depends, however, on the words used, the number of clues needed to guess each one, and the extent to which the teacher discusses props and visual aids after a word has been guessed.

2. The second activity—poem

Ms. Freeman: The next thing we are going to do today is say our "Good Morning" poem. We've recited this poem quite a few times, and I know you know it pretty well. I'm going to take the felt animals out of my folder, and you can help me get the animals

on our flannel board in the right order. [She pulls the felt board closer as she speaks and takes the felt animals out of their folder.] Which animal does the poem speak about first?

Children: The duck!

Ms. Freeman: Yes, the downy duck. So, I'll put the

downy duck up on our flannel board. Which animal comes next in our poem? Which comes second, after the duck?

Luis: The mouse.

Michelle: The dog.

Ana: The bird.

Ms. Freeman: The timid mouse comes second, so I'll put our mouse up on the flannel board. And then the dog with the curly hair comes after the mouse in the poem. [She puts the dog on the flannel board.] And, then, last of all . . .

Children: The bird!

Ms. Freeman: Yes, the scarlet bird, the bird that is a very deep red color. [She puts the bird up on the board.] Okay, now we have the animals all lined up in order, and we are ready to say our poem.

She begins to recite the poem, and points to each animal in order on the board as each new stanza starts. The children join her in reciting the poem.

Ms. Freeman: All of you know this poem so well that next time we say it, I'm going to change something.

Sam: Now?

Ms. Freeman: Oh, no, not today. I'm going to change it when we say it again tomorrow.

Sam: What are you going to do?

Ms. Freeman: I'm going to add something to the felt animals tomorrow. You know the poem so well now that I thought I'd add something new.

Maria: What?

Ms. Freeman: Well, I'm going to write some words from the poem on strips of paper.

Maria: What words?

Ms. Freeman: The animal sounds from the poem: "quack-quack-quack" and "cheep-cheep-cheep" and so on.

Sam: What are you going to do with the animals?

Ms. Freeman: We'll use them again, just the same way. But I'm going to *add* some paper strips with the animal sound words on them.

3. The third activity—song

Ms. Freeman: Okay, next we are going to sing "Head, Shoulders, Knees, and Toes." But, before we start,

I want to explain how we're going to do the song this time.

Remember the other day when I first showed you the chart for this song, this one with the drawings of the two children? [She points to the chart, which shows drawings of a child from the front and the back, with body parts identified by stick-on labels.] We have been using just this drawing [points to the drawing of the child facing front].

Rashid: Where's the words for the eyes and mouth?

Ms. Freeman: Oh, you noticed that they are missing today. I was just about to explain why. Only the labels *head, shoulders, knees, toes,* and *nose* are in place today. [She points to each body part label as she reads it.] I didn't use the labels for the eyes [points to the eyes in the drawing], the ears [points], or the mouth [points].

Rashid: Why not? There's more down there. [He points to the unused labels (*eyes, ears, mouth*), which the teacher has stuck off to the side on the chart.]

Ms. Freeman: Because we are using some new body parts in our song today. We are going to label two of those parts on the drawing of the child facing front, and two of them on the drawing of the child from the back.

Everybody reach around to feel your back. Put your fingers on the middle of your lower back, like this. [She reaches behind her back and turns around so that the children can see.] Bend over just a little bit and feel the bones that are in the middle of your back. That's your spine. Do you feel the bones in your spine?

Children: Yes . . . no . . .

Ms. Freeman: Your spine is right in the middle of your back, and the bones go all the way up and down your back, from your neck to your tailbone. Keep moving your fingers until you feel those bumpy little bones if you haven't found them already. Okay, this word right here on our chart [turns and attaches the label on the chart] says *spine*. So that's one new body part we are singing about today.

The second new body part we will sing about is our *heels* [touches one of hers]. You have two heels, one at the back of each foot. It's this part, right here [cups her hand around the back of her shoe]. . . . That's your ankle, Jason. Your heel is actually inside your shoe, below your ankle. Your heel is the back part of your foot. Right there.

Jason: Oh! I found mine.

Sarah: I found it, too!

Ms. Freeman: Here's the label that says *heels* [attaches it to the chart], and there are two lines going from the label to the drawing, one to the heel of each foot.

Okay, we have one more new body part to sing about today. It's part of our face, so we need to use the drawing that shows the *front* view of the child's body. Here's the new label I've attached to this drawing for today, and the line from the label to the drawing goes right up to here [traces line with finger up to the cheek area of the drawing's face]. What do we call this part of our face? [She points to her own cheek.]

Ana: Chin?

Jamie: Cheek.

Michelle: The side.

Ms. Freeman: This is our chin, down here, below our mouth [touches hers a couple of times] . . . I was pointing a little higher up on my face [taps her cheek again].

Children: Cheek!

Ms. Freeman: Yes, we call this part of our face our cheek, and we have two, don't we? One here [points to one], and one here [points to the other]. I labeled just one cheek on the drawing, and the word is right here [points].

The label *nose* is still on our chart today, isn't it? So, we are going to use that body part again. But we are not using *eyes, ears,* or *mouth.* We are using *spine, heels,* and *cheek* instead [points to each one again on the drawing]. But we'll start the way we always do, with "Head, Shoulders, Knees, and Toes." Okay, stand up, please. Let's go.

She starts to sing and perform the motions, and the children join in. She slows the pace considerably for the middle verse, in which the new body parts' names are embedded, and points slowly and deliberately to these parts of her body.

Rashid: Are we going to do it fast now?

Ms. Freeman: Sure, we can do the first part fast, and then let's slow down for the new part. It's hard to reach around to touch our spine, then down to touch our heels, and then up to our face to do our cheek and nose. In the original version of

our song, all of the body parts for this part of the song were on our face, weren't they? *Eyes* [points], *ears* [points], *mouth,* and *nose.* But now, they are spread out on our body, and we must reach all the way around to our spine on our back, and then down to our heels. So, we'll do the new verse slowly, and do the other parts very, very fast. Let's go. . . .

The class repeats the song, faster this time.

Ms. Freeman: Okay, that was terrific. Please sit back down. [She remains standing.] Now, I'm going to move this chart stand out of our way and pull the flannel board over here again. We'll need it for the next activity.

Maria: What is it?

Ms. Freeman: You will know in just a minute. First I need to take the felt pieces out of this folder.

4. The fourth activity—song

Ms. Freeman: Here's the farmer . . . [places a felt farmer on the flannel board].

Children: BINGO!

Ms. Freeman: . . . and here's the farmer's dog. You are right that we are going to sing "BINGO." We'll need the BINGO letters, and you can say the names of the letters with me as I put them up. Here's the first one [puts the letter *B,* on the flannel board] . . . B . . . the second letter in *BINGO* is . . .

Ms. Freeman and children: The letter *I!*

She continues placing the rest of the letters on the board, and the children recite them along with her.

Ms. Freeman: Okay, we're ready to sing.

She starts singing, and points to each letter as it is named in the song. Before each verse begins, she quickly turns over another letter.

Ms. Freeman: Usually, I put the farmer and dog away after we finish using them for the song, and I show you each letter before I put it back in my folder, and you name them again, don't you?

Children: Yes.

Ms. Freeman: Well, today, we're going to do something different, something we've never done before. We won't need the farmer or the dog anymore, so I'll put them back in my folder. But we do need the letters for our "BINGO" song, so

I'll turn them all over again, so we can see them. There's *B*, and *I*, and *N* . . .

Children: . . . B . . . I . . . N . . .

Sam: . . . G . . . O . . . [Sam recalls the rest of the sequence from memory, and begins to name the next letter before the teacher has turned it over].

Ms. Freeman: . . . then *G*, and last of all, *O*. I brought some more letters, too. I brought *S, W, T,* and *P.*

She places the new letters together on the flannel board as she names them. They are placed low on the board, under the line of letters spelling *BINGO.*

Sarah: What are you going to do with them?

Ms. Freeman: I'll show you. I'm going to replace the *B* in *BINGO* with *T*. The word doesn't say *BINGO* anymore, it says [points to the *T* and sounds it out] /T/ . . . *TINGO.*

She changes the letters again, making the nonsense words *WINGO, PINGO,* and *SINGO.* Each time she changes the letter she reads the word by sounding out the letters. Most children chime in after she sounds out the first one. A few children seem to be reading the new word, right along with the teacher, sounding the initial letter out themselves, as the teacher does.

Ms. Freeman: So, if we change the first letter in a word, we make a different word. Isn't that interesting?

Maria: Cool!

5. The fifth activity—book

Ms. Freeman: The last thing we'll do today is read a book. We haven't read this book before. It's a new one. Let's look at the cover for just a minute.

The class reads and discusses the book *The Doorbell Rang*, by Pat Hutchins (see Box 5.3 on the next page for this first reading of the predictable-text book).

Ms. Freeman: Okay, children, that's all the time we have today for our circle activities. When I call your name, please walk over to your cubby and put on the sweater or jacket you wore to preschool today. It's chilly outside.

Maximizing the instructional power of circle time activities

Now that we've gone through circle time in Ms. Freeman's class, let's take a closer look at the class's activities. After children gathered on the rug, the teacher led them in their first activity, singing "The More We Get Together." This song is one of three songs that the teacher typically chooses from to begin circle time. These songs (about friendship, greeting others, and starting a new day) signal the beginning of circle time and alert the children that it's time to focus.

Singing "The More We Get Together" is a good way to start circle time, as its comforting familiarity eases the transition into this phase of the day. This fairly straightforward song does not require further examination, but there are many other circle time activities that can be presented in a variety of ways in order to enrich children's learning. Such activities can be implemented at a number of different levels, ranging from basic to highly enriched. The higher levels provide more instructional opportunities, and thus have more potential to expand both the range and depth of children's learning. Here, we will discuss several levels of implementation, using Ms. Freeman's circle time activities as examples.

The "Good-Morning" poem

The poem "Good-Morning," by Muriel Sipe, describes someone meeting and greeting four different animals. The poem's four stanzas have four lines each, and the first, third, and fourth lines use a repetitive sentence frame into which a few new words are inserted. The last words in the second and fourth lines always rhyme. Here is the first verse (with the parts that change underlined):

> One day I saw a <u>downy duck</u>,
> With feathers on his back;
> I said, "Good-morning, <u>downy duck</u>,"
> And he said, "<u>Quack, quack, quack</u>."

As with many poems, this one exposes children to rich vocabulary, complex language, and rhyme. The rhyming words help to sensitize children to

sounds within words—in this case, to the rime portions of syllables. (In *back* and *quack*, 'ack' is the rime portion.) This poem's structure helps children remember the words. Children can recite it after having heard it only a few times.

Three levels of implementation for this poem are discussed on the next page, as are follow-up activities that can take place during center time. These follow-up activities integrate the curriculum across multiple classroom learning contexts, which serves to further enhance children's exposure to and understanding of the key ideas presented.

Box 5.3

The Doorbell Rang: Synopsis and guidance for a first reading

Synopsis

In this story, Victoria and Sam's mother gives them some freshly baked cookies, which she tells them to share. Sam and Victoria count the cookies, and figure out that there are enough cookies for them to have six each. But before they can eat the cookies, the doorbell rings. Their friends Tom and Hannah are at the door, and Sam and Victoria's mother invites them to come in and share the cookies. Soon, the doorbell rings again, and two more children arrive. When the doorbell rings a third time, six more children arrive.

Sam, Victoria, and the other children are finally able to distribute the cookies to each child, and there are enough for just one cookie per child. But before they can begin eating their cookies, the doorbell rings one last time. The children look reluctant, knowing that sharing cookies now would require someone to give up part of a cookie. To everyone's relief, Sam and Victoria's grandmother is at the door—with a large tray of freshly baked cookies.

The book features predictable text patterned around the visitors' arrivals, the mother's responses, and the sharing of the cookies.

Reading the book

To introduce the book before she reads it to the class, Ms. Freeman reads the title and author's name, then comments on the cover illustration, which shows a large number of children gathered at the inside of the front door. The teacher points out that one child

is peeking through the door's mail slot, and that the other children look very interested in what he sees outside.

Because the children in the class have no idea what this could be, Ms. Freeman decides to wonder out loud about the scenario, then start reading the story right away, rather than ask the children what they think the child on the cover sees. Ms. Freeman says,

> The children inside the house seem very interested in knowing who is outside the door. I wonder who's there? Let's read the story and find out.

She supports the children's comprehension by reading expressively, pointing out relevant details in the illustrations, and commenting occasionally about story events. She asks a couple of well-positioned questions: "What do you think the children are thinking about their cookies now?" and "What do you think they will do if more children arrive?"

She also stresses the predictable-text refrains in the book (e.g., "'Come in,' said Ma" and "No one makes cookies like Grandma") and encourages the children to say them along with her when they have become familiar.

After reading the story, Ms. Freeman prompts a brief discussion, focusing on the story's main theme of sharing. When the discussion ends, the teacher tells the children that the next day during small group time, they will figure out exactly how Sam and Victoria divided the cookies each time that more children arrived.

The *basic level* of implementation for the "Good-Morning" poem consists of little more than its recitation by the teacher and the children. Felt pieces depicting the four animals featured in the poem provide physical support, helping children to identify each animal. When first introducing the poem, the teacher explains that four animals are in the poem, and names them as their felt representations are placed on the flannel board in a line:

> This is the downy duck. This is the timid mouse. This is the curly dog, and this is the scarlet bird. Now, I'll say the poem for you.

As she recites the poem for the first time, she points to each animal in turn; in some parts, she also performs accompanying actions (e.g., bending over at the waist for greeting the dog, yawning and stretching for waking up the bird). She uses gestures and an expressive voice to convey what it means for the mouse to be "timid" and "meek."

The teacher then invites the children to join in on the second recitation. The pace is a bit slower this time to support their participation. The poem is repeated several times a week, across several weeks. The children gradually learn all of the poem's words, and are able to recite it with ease.

In the *enriched level* of implementation, the sound words (*quack*, *squeak*, and so on) are printed out and glued to strips of felt. Ms. Freeman tells the children about this change the day before she implements it. Teachers often alert children to an upcoming change in a familiar activity. It's useful, however, not to reveal all of the details when first mentioning a change, as children will become curious and ask questions to get more details if only a little bit is revealed. Asking questions fosters conversation and critical thinking and is beneficial for the development of children's oral language and cognition.

On the day Ms. Freeman changes the activity, she asks the children whether they remember what she told them the day before—that she was going to introduce new materials for the "Good-Morning" poem. The children do remember, so Ms. Freeman has the class identify each felt animal,

then she shows them the new word strips of the animal sounds. She reads each word strip, and with the children's help she places each one next to the correct animal. Then, the class once again recites "Good-Morning"; this time, Ms. Freeman points to the felt animals *and* the appropriate sound cards as the poem progresses.

After using these materials for a few weeks, Ms. Freeman again changes the activity. The *highly enriched level* increases opportunities for children to develop their literacy skills. As before, she alerts the children to the change the day prior. For the highly enriched version of the activity, Ms. Freeman writes out the poem's title in big print on the top of a large piece of chart paper, with the lines of the poem below it (see illustration). Each stanza has a small picture of its corresponding animal next to it. The animals' names (e.g., "downy duck") and their sounds (e.g., "Quack, quack, quack") are written on removable tag board strips, which are attached to the poem chart with self-sticking fabric. After using the poem chart with the children several times with all of the words in place, Ms. Freeman removes these strips, leaving the spaces on the chart blank.

At the next circle time, she asks the children to help her put the animals' names and sounds in their correct places in the poem. By this time, most of the children have no doubt that the first stanza is about a duck—and if they need help, the picture of the duck beside the first line of the poem reminds them. They easily recall that the duck's sound words are "Quack, quack, quack." Their experience with the animal sounds on the tag board strips, in conjunction with the animal felt pieces, makes the children confident about their knowledge of the poem and helps them begin identifying words.

From now on, before reciting the poem, the class reviews the word strips in order. Ms. Freeman helps the children sound out the first few letters of each sound word. As the class recites the poem together, the teacher points to the words for each animal's name and sound.

Ms. Freeman always reads the title before the class recites the "Good-Morning" poem. Over time, as children become more familiar with the alphabet letters and the sounds they represent, she begins to hold her finger briefly on the first letter of each word in the poem's title, rather than moving it quickly to underline the whole word. This pointing gives children time to connect the letter they see at the beginning of each word with the sound they hear their teacher make as she reads. She then underlines the rest of the word in a continuous sweep. In time, Ms. Freeman will linger on additional letters in some words, such as the *d* at the end of *good* and the *n* in the middle of *morning*.

Teachers can also create several small "books" of the poem for children to follow up with during center time. To make these, fold a sturdy piece of cardstock or poster board in half, print the title and the author's name on the front, and print the basic sentence frame of the poem on the inside, leaving blank spaces for the animals' names and sounds in the first, third, and fourth lines of each stanza. This format creates a replica of the chart the children have been using during circle time. The animals' names and sounds are printed on small poster board

strips and backed with small pieces of self-sticking fabric, so they can easily be placed on the blank spaces. The words can either be set out on a small flannel board next to the books or included with the books on a stapled-in flap of felt or paper backed with self-sticking fabric. The book and the adhesive words can be laminated for extra strength.

To add extra challenges over time, the teacher can insert additional pages that leave different spaces in the poem blank. For example, a second page might have blanks and corresponding word strips for "one day" (the first words of the first line) and "good-morning" (the words in the middle of the third line). Later, the teacher might even add a third page of the poem, which leaves out different words. In the end, each additional page presents the poem with different words missing.

When implementing this extension of the highly enriched activity, the teacher gauges whether some of the children are interested and ready for these challenges. The children's experience with the chart and removable words used at circle time will prepare many of them to use the small books during center time, and the teacher may encourage particular children to use the books based on their

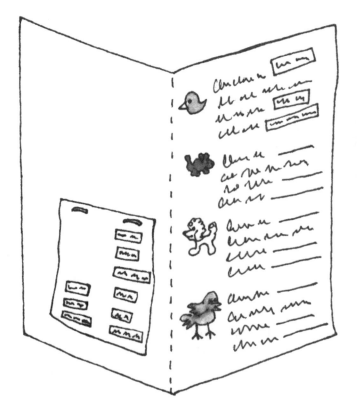

current level of literacy skill. Teachers can use small group time to introduce the additional pages, which omit different words. Children might need this initial instructional support before using the new book pages independently.

But during circle time, a teacher should first and foremost strive to help preschoolers enjoy and understand the poem. Accompanying the poem with physical actions and props (such as the felt pieces) may help. However, the teacher should avoid an overemphasis on the printed words in the beginning, as it may decrease the children's comprehension of the poem's meaning.

The overall purpose of using additional materials, such as the chart and the poem books, is to draw children's attention to individual words in the poem, helping them begin to use and understand print and sound features. These experiences facilitate *fingerpoint* reading, when a child points to printed words while reciting text memorized from hearing it read aloud. Some children are able to do this by the later preschool years, though not all can, as children vary a lot in their interactions with print, and thus in their print knowledge. Research indicates that fingerpoint reading does not develop simply from memorizing a poem and seeing a teacher point to each word as the poem is recited (Ehri & Sweet 1991). Rather, fingerpoint reading requires skill in recognizing and naming letters, the ability to isolate the first phoneme of spoken words, and the realization that an isolated sound in a spoken word can and must be linked to a letter or a combination of letters.

Many preschool experiences help children to build this literacy skill base. The use of a poem chart with removable words, as described earlier, does help children attend to some print details as a teacher provides guidance. This guided experience supports children in developing and deploying literacy skills in an authentic reading context.

A teacher can follow the same basic procedure used for "Good-Morning" with a number of other poems that might typically be used in circle time throughout the year. By year's end, a classroom's collection of small books related to poems might number five or six.

The "Head, Shoulders, Knees, and Toes" song

In the well-known song "Head, Shoulders, Knees, and Toes," children stand to sing and perform accompanying actions. Children first reach up to touch their heads and shoulders, one time each, and then bend down to touch their knees and then their toes, repeating the sequence two times. This series of motions is repeated before a verse in the middle directs children to their eyes, ears, mouth, and nose. In the final verse, children again touch their heads, shoulders, knees, and toes. Like Ms. Freeman did, teachers can creatively vary the song to include different body parts. This song provides physical activity, helps children learn the names of body parts, and exposes children to rhyme (an important part of phonological awareness).

At a *basic level* of implementation, the teacher leads the children in singing and performing the accompanying actions. The song can be included in circle time activities once or twice a week, and can be repeated several times within a single circle time session. For example, the song can be sung once at a moderate speed, once very fast, and once very slow. In addition to providing more exercise for the children, repetition at varying speeds reinforces the meanings of the words *fast* and *slow*. After introducing children to the song and these variations, the teacher might ask children on later occasions whether they want to sing the song again very quickly or very slowly. On other occasions, the teacher might specify a sequence of speeds to follow.

The *enriched level* of this activity includes new verses that introduce more body terminology, substituting, for example, *cheek*, *spine*, *heels*, *elbow*, *kneecap*, and *neck* for the standard body parts. This approach works best with props—in Ms. Freeman's case, a chart with two large drawings of a child from the front and the back, with detachable labels for the body parts. The class might sing the song once with the standard verses, then once again with the new words.

Before singing the new version, the teacher should point to his or her own body to introduce the new body parts, then ask the children to locate them on their own bodies, as we saw Ms. Freeman do earlier when she introduced *spine*, *heels*, and *cheek*. The teacher then points out these body parts on the drawing of the child's body and highlights their word labels. Just a few new body parts are introduced at a time. Each new version might be used two or three times over the course of a few weeks before a different version is introduced.

For the *highly enriched level* of this activity, which we saw Ms. Freeman demonstrate, the teacher uses drawings of both the front and the back of a child's body. When introducing the activity, the teacher points to and names each new body part on her own body and asks children to find each part on their own bodies. She then shows the label, reads it, and attaches it to the appropriate blank line on the chart. The new body parts and the discussions that follow from their introduction increases children's vocabulary and concept learning.

Follow-up activities for use during center time can be added, as well. For example, using poster board, the teacher makes small books with miniature versions of the diagrams and printed labels to match. The pages and the word labels can be laminated. The pages are secured with a metal ring binder. If desired, the teacher can insert an additional page with a picture of a human skeleton. Lines might be drawn from different body parts, and printed labels for these parts can be provided.

The "BINGO" song

In the first verse of "BINGO," a well-known song about a farmer's dog, the letters of the dog's name are spelled out three successive times:

> There was a farmer had a dog
> And BINGO was his name-o.
> *B-I-N-G-O, B-I-N-G-O, B-I-N-G-O,*
> BINGO was his name-o.

In the remaining verses, one letter at a time is removed and substituted with a clap. No letters at all are named in the last verse; instead, there

are only claps. This song exposes children to letter names and the importance of letter order, it requires children to synchronize a movement (clapping) with a song's rhythm, and it exposes children to a growth pattern.

A *basic level* of instruction for "BINGO" is the oral version of the song, which the teacher leads. The teacher also models the clapping that replaces the letters that are left out as the verses are repeated. Though this basic level of implementation is a great starting point, the song can provide much deeper levels of learning.

In a *slightly enriched level* of implementation, the teacher uses a flannel board with felt pieces representing the farmer, the dog, and the letters in *BINGO*. Before singing the song, the teacher introduces these pieces and places them on the board. The teacher points to the farmer, the dog, and to each letter as it is named in the first verse. Before singing each subsequent verse, the teacher removes the letters that are *not* sung and replaces them with pictures of clapping hands. In the *enriched level* of implementation, the teacher introduces additional letters after the children sing the song through completely. The teacher replaces the felt letters, making the word *BINGO* visible again. Then, the teacher replaces the *B* with other letters (as Ms. Freeman did with the letters *S*, *W*, *T*, and *P*). She then reads the new nonsense words (e.g., *SINGO*, *WINGO*, *TINGO*) with the children.

In a *highly enriched level* of this activity, the teacher removes letters from *BINGO* and reads the words that result. For example, the teacher might remove *G* and *O*; the remaining word is *BIN*. The teacher reads this word with the children, commenting that *BINGO* without the *GO* is *BIN*. Next, the teacher might remove the *B* from *BIN* and say, "Now the word is just *IN*." The teacher can create a few different words each time the children sing "BINGO" during circle time, deleting letters both from the beginning of the word (e.g.,

BIN changed to *IN*) and from the end (e.g., *BINGO* changed to *BIN*). Substituting different consonants for the *B* in *BINGO* also provides new opportunities for creating and manipulating words (e.g., *BINGO* changed to *TINGO*; *TIN* changed to *IN*).

The highly enriched version can also include follow-up activities for use during small group or center time, which will extend and reinforce the instruction received in circle time. One activity involves creating and changing words with magnetic letters or letter tiles. Children are likely to imitate initial consonant substitutions introduced during circle time, and some may read the words created. They are also likely to compose new letter combinations. Children can sound out these "words"—some of which may be nonsense, some real—along with their teacher. Children often find this activity enjoyable, and it helps them learn about letters, their sequence, and sounds.

The "The Doorbell Rang" book

In this predictable-text book by Pat Hutchins, the math concept of dividing a quantity into parts is central to the plot. Such a book may require additional materials to support children's learning; otherwise, they are unlikely to fully grasp the book's math concept.

Circle time is a good setting for a first reading of the book. But Ms. Freeman plans to explore the book more extensively during small group time, which will best accommodate the use of concrete materials to demonstrate this story's events. A small group setting also is necessary for the level of engagement required for children to help solve the math problems the book poses. Chapter 6, which focuses on the small group learning context, details a follow-up reading of *The Doorbell Rang*, in which its math concepts are supported more explicitly through demonstrations and discussions.

◆　◆　◆

As this chapter has illustrated, circle time is an appropriate context to provide a variety of unique instructional activities at increasingly richer levels to support children's learning of oral language, literacy, and math concepts and skills. Circle time activities can also set the stage for experiences in other parts of the preschool day, including center time and small group time, which is the focus of Chapter 6.

Reflection questions

1. Why should teachers alternate the types of activities children engage in during circle time? How can this best be done to support learning across multiple content domains?

2. Ms. Freeman introduces five activities during circle time. How does she plan to extend the concepts introduced in these activities into other learning contexts?

3. What follow-up activities would *you* plan to accompany "BINGO" or *The Doorbell Rang*?

4. How does varying the levels of instructional implementation (from basic to highly enriched) lead to greater integration of learning?

6

Integration in Teacher-Organized Small Group Time

Throughout the preschool day, there are many occasions when children divide into small groups—formally and informally, on their own and at the teacher's direction. Children sit in small groups during snack and mealtimes; they gather naturally in small groups during center/choice time; and in some programs, they are organized for activities by the teacher during scheduled small group time, which is separate from center time. While the opportunities for learning in all three settings contribute to the same general goals, the social roles, relationships, and the instructional strategies are different in each.

During center/choice time, children initiate and direct much of their play and learning. Group size and composition change dynamically throughout each center time period as children make choices from among the variety of activities. While many of the instructional concerns regarding center time and teacher-organized small groups overlap, each nevertheless deserves separate consideration. Chapter 7 will be devoted to center/choice time.

During snack and mealtimes, even when teachers assign children in small groups to specific tables, eating takes center stage, which decreases the range of instructional opportunities. Eating, however, is accompanied by conversations covering a broad range of topics, many of which

are directly related to children's experiences at the table. The conversations also frequently involve *decontextualized* talk, which is talk about the past or the future as opposed to the here and the now. Decontextualized talk is often rich in content; and it requires children to pay more attention to the language they hear and use, given that the immediate physical environment (*context*) cannot be consulted to aid comprehension (Dickinson, McCabe, & Clark-Chiarelli 2004).

Clearly, these informal groupings formed by teachers around eating are a rich venue for social interaction and can present rich learning opportunities. But because the learning context of *small group time* is still widely underutilized in preschool programs, we will focus on it primarily. This chapter, then, explores how teachers can schedule and organize a period of planned small group activities to implement effective and powerful instruction and integrate content with other learning contexts.

Logistics of small groups

Teachers assign children to groups for teacher-organized small group time. In each small group session, the teacher typically addresses specific goals by planning a focused activity. Over sessions, a range of goals is addressed. Children actively participate and often explore concrete materials. But, unlike in center and other small group times, children are not presented with a range of activities or topics from which they choose. Rather, the teacher chooses and plans the activity for each session and guides children's engagement directly and explicitly to meet specific goals. A teacher's responsiveness to children during small group time consists of adjusting instructional approaches, content level, and feedback to respond to each child's understanding of the topic or activity at hand. The smaller the group size, the better a teacher can meet individual needs.

Because the size of a small group determines how much individual guidance and support a teacher can actually provide, teachers often try to limit the number of children in a small group to four or five. However, given the typical preschool class staffing of just two adults for as many as 20 children, it is difficult to create groupings of this size. In some programs, one teacher pulls out a small group of children during center/choice time to work with them on a planned and directed activity. This approach is less than ideal, as it decreases the staffing available for the majority of children who are engaged in center time activities and reduces the extent to which adults can support and enrich children's play. This approach also places the directed small group activity in an environment that may be distracting to the children in the small group.

It often works better to designate a separate, teacher-organized small group time, during which all the children work on planned activities in small groupings of four or five each. Variations on that format are the focus of this chapter. A dedicated small group time allows for a higher level of teacher interaction than is possible in the center time scenario, when a teacher must supervise and support children throughout the classroom in as many as eight different centers. A separate small group time can also help teachers address the common center time concern that children often favor one or two of the centers more than the others. Teachers are often reluctant to assign children to specific centers, because this violates the important center time principle of allowing children to make their own choices. At the same time, teachers understand that each center provides unique opportunities for learning, and that children with narrow preferences may miss out on important experiences and learning.

A dedicated small group time, however, still must solve the staffing challenge of 20 children and only two teachers. Teachers sometimes plan one activity for just four or five children, which is directed and supported by one teacher, and then provide two or three other small group activities that require less support for the rest of the class, which the other teacher monitors. Although the two or three secondary activities are venues for somewhat independent engagement, this scenario still allows for a higher level of teacher interaction than is possible when a teacher must supervise and support children in many centers throughout the classroom during center time.

The more independent small group activities that run parallel to the primary small group can include some materials taken from centers, such as puzzles, playdough, construction toys, writing tools and paper, and small sets of blocks for tabletop use. Some arts and crafts projects are also suitable for the independent small group activities. Their use in these small groups can help familiarize children with a range of activities and help build new interests, which are likely to expand the center time choices they make.

To keep group sizes small (ideally limited to four or five children) teachers sometimes rotate groups through a planned series of small group activities across the span of a whole week. Group composition is usually stable for an extended period of time, perhaps for as long as four to six weeks. Then, a teacher reevaluates and regroups for the next four to six weeks, basing decisions on social considerations and children's learning needs. Teachers can post current group assignments on a chart displayed in the classroom.

The role of teacher-organized small groups

Each small group setting has a unique social and instructional role in a comprehensive preschool program. By including a small group time in the daily schedule, a teacher has more options to situate learning in a suitable context and can reduce the risk of undermining goals in one domain to support goals in another. Sometimes teacher-organized small group time is used to follow up on an activity introduced in a previous whole group context. At other times a concept or skill is introduced in small groups before related activities are provided in center time for children's independent use.

Small group settings, used in combination with whole group settings and center time, give teachers additional opportunities for integrating learning both within and across domains.

Following up on previous book readings

As mentioned in Chapter 5, Ms. Freeman read the storybook *The Doorbell Rang* during circle time and planned to follow up the reading with additional exploration during small group time. A small group setting is a good context for reviewing a story or a concept in greater depth with children, as the teacher can interact more closely with the children, can better gauge their comprehension, and can more easily adjust prompts and feedback to meet individual needs. A small group setting also offers greater opportunity than a whole group setting for individual participation. Each of the small groups participates in the follow-up activity within a few days of the original story reading.

As previously discussed, *The Doorbell Rang* is a story about sharing, in which two children, Sam and Victoria, must divide twelve cookies among the increasingly larger group of friends who decide to visit. Children have no difficulty understanding that in order to be fair, each person must have the same number of cookies, but dividing a quantity of items into equal groups is still pretty abstract for preschoolers.

Using manipulatives as props helps to reinforce the division concepts the teacher introduced during story time. In the small group setting, the teacher can focus on math details very explicitly, using additional materials and considerable discussion and demonstration to support the children's understanding of dividing. Now, we'll take a look at how Ms. Freeman uses an activity during small group time to foster children's understanding of this book.

In this activity, Ms. Freeman and four children reenact the division of cookies in *The Doorbell Rang*, using a flannel board and felt pieces representing the cookies and the children in the story. Earlier, when preparing the props, Ms. Freeman made twelve simple cookies out of tan felt circles with black dots representing chocolate chips, as well as twelve children's faces out of tan and brown felt ovals, with drawn-on eyes, noses, and mouths, and yarn for hair.

She begins by holding up the book and engaging the children in a very brief review of Sam and Victoria's problem and their solution. Then, she explains that they will read the story again, this time with the children figuring out how Sam and Victoria divided the cookies among their growing group of visitors. She holds the felt cookies on her lap on one paper plate and the faces on another.

After reading the first page, Ms. Freeman places two faces, representing Sam and Victoria, on the left-hand side of the flannel board. She then reads the next page, where Sam and Victoria say they can each have six cookies. Ms. Freeman and the children count as she places six felt cookies beside Sam's "face," and six beside Victoria's. The small group's discussion and reenactment of the story after this point went like this:

Ms. Freeman: Now the situation in the story changes, doesn't it? Do Sam and Victoria really get to eat six cookies each?

Children: No!

Ms. Freeman: No, they don't, because something happens . . .

Michelle: The doorbell ranged and ranged.

Jason: Too many kids came.

Keisha: But their grandma brought more.

Ms. Freeman: That's right. The doorbell rang again and again, and more and more children came in. Their grandma did come at the very end of the story, and she brought a lot more cookies. But before their grandma arrived, Sam and Victoria's mother kept telling the new children that they could share the cookies. So, Sam and Victoria had to keep dividing them.

We're going to figure out how Sam and Victoria knew how many cookies each child would have. I'll turn the page to help us remember which children came first. [She reads a line of text.] "It was Tom and Hannah from next door." I'll put up these two felt faces for Tom and Hannah. Now, what do Sam and Victoria do with their cookies?

Luis: Give some to the other kids. Share them.

Ms. Freeman: Yes, they shared their cookies. They are very thoughtful children. They shared their cookies so that each of them would have the same number of cookies. I wonder how they did that—how they figured out how many cookies each of them would have? Does anyone have an idea?

Michelle: They took one of those cookies and gave it to that friend, and then took one and gave it to that friend, and then another one and gave it to that one, and then another one to that one.

Michelle points to the flannel board, indicating that one cookie at a time was taken from Sam's group of cookies and then from Victoria's for each new child. Michelle stops after suggesting that two cookies each be moved from Sam's group and Victoria's group to those of Tom and Hannah.

Ms. Freeman: Yes, we could move cookies one at a time from Sam and Victoria to Tom and Hannah. I'll do that on the flannel board.

Ms. Freeman repeats Michelle's directions and moves the felt cookies. This leaves four cookies in Sam's group, four in Victoria's, and two each for Tom and Hannah.

Ms. Freeman: Let's take a look at this. Do you think Sam and Victoria stopped sharing their cookies at this point?

Keisha: That's not fair. Sam and Victoria have more cookies.

Luis: They have only two cookies, and they have . . . 1, 2, 3, 4. [Luis uses his fingers to count the cookies beside Sam's and Victoria's faces.]

Ms. Freeman: You are right. All of the children don't yet have the same number of cookies. What would happen if I took one more cookie from Sam, and gave it to Hannah, and took one more cookie from Victoria, and gave it to Tom?

Luis: Hannah would have, umm, she would have, umm . . . three cookies.

Ms. Freeman: Yes, she would. What about Sam? How many cookies would he have left?

Luis: Umm, he would have, umm . . . 1, 2, 3, 4. [He points in the air toward the flannel board with his finger.]

Ms. Freeman: Sam has four cookies now [points]. But if he gave one to Hannah, how many would he have left? [She begins removing one felt cookie from Sam's row of four.]

Children: Three!

Ms. Freeman: Yes, three. [She moves a felt cookie from Sam's row to Hannah's.]

Jason: And if you give one more to that one [points to Tom's cookies], then there will be three left up there [points to Victoria's cookies].

Ms. Freeman: Yes, I'll do that right now [moves cookie]. Now, each child has three cookies. They all have the same number of cookies. That's fair, isn't it?

Keisha: Yes, it's fair when you all have the same cookies.

Ms. Freeman: They have the same number of cookies, yes, and that's a fair way to share. But, before they can eat their cookies, what happens?

Keisha: More kids came.

Sam: The doorbell went off again.

Ms. Freeman: Yes, the doorbell rang again. This time, "It was Peter and his little brother." [She reads from the book.] The mother invites them in, and tells Victoria and Sam, "You can share the cookies."

Ms. Freeman and the small group continue the follow-up activity in this fashion. They review each new arrival in the book, and then they reallocate the cookies accordingly. They compare their groupings of the felt cookies with the book's illustrations. Ms. Freeman ends the small group session by telling them that in a few days, after all the children have participated in the small group activity, the flannel board and felt pieces will be available for their use during center time.

Math games

Game formats are a great way to introduce children to math concepts and engage everyone in the group. When presenting math activities to groups of up to five children, teachers can focus intently on comprehension, adjusting the pace of instruction to better suit the small group. Some math activities that are experienced first in a teacher-organized small group setting can then be made available for more independent use in center time. Others may follow up on earlier instruction; for example, activities may explicitly relate to a book the class read, to a curriculum theme (like growth of plants and animals), or to the concepts and skills introduced as part of the math curriculum.

Let's look at another example from Ms. Freeman's classroom. Based on the children's current understanding of geometry, an important area of mathematical learning, Ms. Freeman decides that a shape matching game will be a useful activity. This activity is designed to help young children learn about the properties of different shapes and to recognize these properties across several variations. The children do not need to have mastered the recognition of any particular shapes before playing this game, as it is designed to build this skill.

The children have probably already gained basic knowledge of shapes from a variety of contexts, such as books, play with tangram materials, and games involving shapes (Clements

1999, 2004). (For a few suggestions of books about shapes and other mathematical topics, see Appendix A, "Math-Related Children's Books.")

In all of these experiences, or at least across a range of experiences, children should be exposed to a variety of triangles, rectangles with different length-height ratios, and more complex shapes. For example, shapes with four straight sides that are not rectangles should be included (such as non-rectangular parallelograms and trapezoids), as should shapes with more than four straight sides (such as pentagons and hexagons). Children should also be introduced to the oval.

Experience with many different examples of a shape gradually builds children's understanding that some variations do not change the particular form. For example, there are many different kinds of triangles, although all are similar in having three sides and three corners. Similarly, rectangles vary in the length of their sides, making some very long and thin and others much shorter and fatter. All have in common four straight sides, with opposites parallel, and four square corners. (For more on the importance of variation, see Box 6.1 on the next page.)

Before playing the game, Ms. Freeman gathers materials: a set of twelve cards with a different shape on each one, a large poster (featuring the shapes shown on the cards, with similar shapes located near one another), and a folder or envelope. The cards have the following shapes:

- four triangles (two isosceles triangles, differing in their height-width ratios—one tall and thin, the other short and wide; one equilateral triangle; and one right-angled triangle, with a height-width ratio similar to the taller of the two isosceles triangles);

- five shapes with four sides (one square; one rectangle that is about twice as long as it is high; one rectangle that is about three times longer than it is high; one non-rectangular parallelogram; and one trapezoid);

- one pentagon; one hexagon; and one circle.

Shape cards can be made from index cards or another type of sturdy paper, and each shape can

Box 6.1

Learning through variation

In her book *Beginning to Read*, Marilyn Adams tells this story about her young daughter getting acquainted with letters:

$$\text{G} \quad \text{C} \quad \textbf{G} \quad \text{C} \quad \text{G}$$
$$\text{C} \quad \textbf{G} \quad \textbf{C} \quad \text{G} \quad \text{C}$$

When challenged to name these two letters, my daughter, now just three years old, looked me squarely in the eye and said firmly, "I call them both *C*."

It is not that she could not discriminate their shapes: She regularly performs perfectly on an uppercase letter-matching game on the computer. Nor is she unaware that I like to call these letters by different names: Her answer was clearly intended to preempt the correction that she knew I would produce.

But she has a point. In what reasonable kind of world would people agree to call both a dachshund and a St. Bernard "dogs" while calling one of these characters a "C" and the other a "G"? To us, the answer is obvious: in the kind of world where people use *C*s and *G*s discriminately for reading and writing—which, of course, she does not yet do. (Adams 1990, 345)

Concept learning requires the recognition of similarities across various examples. Though different dogs, for instance, can vary considerably in size, the length of their fur, and so on, each has a set of features that uniquely makes it a dog and not a cat. Infants as young as 5 or 6 months can recognize the features of animals if shown a series of pictures of different kinds of dogs, for example, or different kinds of cats (Eimas & Quinn 1994). Concept learning is also important in letter recognition. For example, children learn to ignore irrelevant variations in letters that are printed in different fonts, and to focus instead on the basic features that distinguish each kind of letter (Schickedanz 1998).

Unlike familiar categories of animals or furniture or plants, some categories of shapes and letters resemble one another so closely that children at first confuse them, thinking they are simply different examples of the same shape or letter rather than distinct shapes or letters. Children learn that lots of very different-looking things are still triangles. At the same time, they must also learn that when a shape they may want to call a *square* has two long sides and two short sides, it is not a square but a *rectangle*. Similarly, many letters, such as the capital letters *E* and *F*, are easily confused, as their similarities outweigh their distinctions.

If children are shown just one example of a shape or letter category, and are not exposed to multiple variations, they are misled into thinking that this particular form is the *only* one that qualifies as the specific shape. Through comparison and discussion, children learn to distinguish one shape or letter from all the others, and they also learn to ignore irrelevant variations found in different examples of the same shape or letter.

---

either be drawn or cut from black construction paper (as shown on the next page) and mounted on the card. The shape should be in the center of the card, and even the smallest shapes should be large enough to be seen easily at a distance. The cards can be laminated to make them last longer.

To introduce the activity, Ms. Freeman explains to the small group that they are going to play a guessing game about shapes. Before playing the game, the children examine the shapes on the cards and compare them with the shapes on the poster.

They find that each shape on a card has a matching shape on the poster; this helps the children begin to think about shapes in terms of their features.

Ms. Freeman: Okay, so now you understand the idea that all of the shapes on these cards [holds up the whole set of cards] are also on the poster. Each card has an exact match someplace up here on the poster. To play the game, I will give a card, hidden in a folder, to one of you, and that child will come to my end of the table and sit in this chair beside me. The child will not show us what shape is on the card. Only the child sitting up here

will be able to look in the folder and see the card. The rest of us will ask questions to get information about the shape, and it is our job to figure out which shape is on the child's card.

Children: Cool! Yeah!

Ms. Freeman: Okay, we'll just take turns in the order that you're sitting. If we don't have time for everyone to have a turn today, you will get a turn the next time we play the game in our small group. I'll keep a list of those who have turns today, so I will be sure to remember who hasn't gotten a turn yet.

I'm going to write Maria's name on my clipboard right now, because she's going to have the first turn. Maria, come sit in the chair beside me. [Maria moves to the chair.]

Ms. Freeman: Here's the folder with a shape card inside. You may open it to look at the shape, but don't let anyone see it, and don't tell us what it is. Take a peek, and then close the folder and don't say a word about what you saw. Just keep it in your own mind.

Maria opens the folder and looks.

Jamie: She should be silent.

Ms. Freeman: Right. She should remain silent about what she sees. Okay, Maria has looked at the

card and closed the folder. She's ready for our first question. Let's ask her if the shape on her card has three sides. I think that might be a good question to start the game.

Rashid: Does it?

Maria shakes her head no.

Ms. Freeman: Do you want to open the folder to double check, or are you sure that you remember what the shape looks like?

Maria: I remember.

Ms. Freeman: Okay, so what do we know about the shape? Let's look at our poster. Can the shape on Maria's card be a triangle? [She gestures toward the triangles mounted on the poster.]

Children: No.

Rashid: They have three sides, and hers doesn't.

Sarah: It's something else with more sides.

Ms. Freeman: Well, it could be a shape with more sides, or it could be a shape with no sides at all.

Maria: It has some sides.

Ana: How many?

Ms. Freeman: That's a good question. Can you answer that, Maria? How many sides does your shape have? You can open the folder and look at the shape again, and count the sides, if you'd like. And we can listen to that, but don't tell us anything else about your shape. Okay? We must guess.

Maria: [She opens the folder to check the shape.] 1, 2, 3, 4. Four sides.

Ms. Freeman: Okay. That's good information. Now, which shapes on our poster do we know are not possible matches?

Ana: It can't be a circle.

Ms. Freeman: Right, a circle doesn't have any sides at all. Which other shapes do we know that it is not?

Rashid: That one. [He points to the hexagon.]

Ms. Freeman: The hexagon, right, because a hexagon has 1, 2, 3, 4, 5, 6 sides . . . more than four, for sure.

Jamie: And not that next one either. [He points toward the pentagon.]

Ms. Freeman: This one, here? Let's see how many sides it has—1, 2, 3, 4, 5. [The children count along with Ms. Freeman as she points to the sides of the shape.] This shape has five sides, and we call it a pentagon. So, you are right. Her shape cannot be a pentagon, because she said that her shape has just four sides. So, it must be one of these shapes up here. [She gestures toward the middle group of shapes, all of which have four sides.]

Sarah: Is it a square?

Ms. Freeman: We could ask that. Maria, did you hear that question? Does your shape have four sides that are all the same length—a square? [Ms. Freeman points to the square on the chart.]

Maria: [She peeks inside the folder to check.] No.

Ms. Freeman: Okay, so it's not a square. Let's think about what we could ask next. Let's ask if all the sides are straight up and down or straight across, and not slanted. I think we need to know whether there are four square corners, or no square corners.

Sarah: Ask that.

Ms. Freeman: Okay. Maria, we want to know whether your shape has sides that are straight up and down or straight across, sides that do not slant like the sides on these two shapes. [She points to the two non-parallel sides of the trapezoid and to the two slanting sides of the parallelogram.]

Maria: They aren't like that.

Ms. Freeman: The sides don't slant?

Maria: No.

Ms. Freeman: So your shape has four square corners?

Maria: Yes.

Ms. Freeman: Okay, which shapes are possibilities? We already know that it's not the square, because someone asked that question earlier. So, we are down to two choices—these two rectangles—right here. [She points out the two remaining rectangles that are possibilities.] Both have sides that are straight up and down or straight across, and both have four square corners. What could we ask to figure out which one Maria has on her card?

Ana: Is it this one [holds her hands pretty far apart] or this one [holds her hands closer together]?

Ms. Freeman: Yes, we could ask if it's the longer one or the shorter one. Go ahead and ask that.

Ana: Is it the long one?

Maria: No.

Ms. Freeman: Okay, which one does Maria have?

Jamie: That one. [He points to the shorter of the two rectangles.] Is that right?

Maria: Yes.

Ms. Freeman: Okay, hold your card up in front of the poster so we can make sure.

Maria holds up her card and shows the class.

Ms. Freeman: Did we guess the right one?

Children: Yes!

Ms. Freeman: Okay, thank you, Maria!

The children continue the game until the end of small group time.

To vary this activity, Ms. Freeman adds new shapes to the collection and mixes the shapes on the poster to create contrasts in properties among the shapes. Other materials such as information books, blocks, and a variety of shape manipulatives (such as magnets or tangrams) are also appropriate for follow-up activities in later small group sessions and during center time.

Additional small group possibilities and considerations

The activities described in detail here are just two examples of the possibilities for teacher-planned small group activities. Other examples for small group time have been mentioned in earlier chapters, as follow-up activities to circle or story time experiences. For example, in Chapter 2, Ms. Freeman introduced measuring activities in a small group context as a follow-up to reading *Inch by Inch*. In Chapter 4, Ms. Freeman planned a follow-up activity for small groups that encouraged children to use pictures of wheeled objects to make a number book based on the format of the book *Ten Black Dots*.

Other activities described in this book can be modified for use during teacher-organized small group time. In Chapter 4, Ms. Freeman told the children about a picture- and word-matching game they could complete in center time as a follow-up activity to reading *One Duck Stuck*. She introduced children to the matching materials in a whole group setting, but she could instead have done this during a planned small group.

Selecting the appropriate context to introduce such activities should be based on children's prior experiences and other considerations, such as time restraints imposed by the day's other activities. In this case, the children had already been exposed to matching printed words and pictures. If the group had less prior experience, or if some of the children needed additional support (e.g., mixed age groups, English language learners, children with special needs), a small group setting rather than a whole group circle time would have been more effective. Even the second reading of *One Duck Stuck*—demonstrated in Chapter 4 in a whole group setting—might work better in a teacher-organized small group for some groups of children.

◆　◆　◆

The length of the preschool day and the particular classroom staffing will affect whether a teacher will be able to schedule a separate teacher-organized small group time. If time and staffing permit, this context can be used strategically to extend prior experiences or to introduce something new to contribute to children's overall learning. In the next chapter, we will consider how center time, another important learning context, also uses the principles of integration to support children's learning.

Reflection questions

1. How and why should teachers organize and lead the small groups described in this chapter?

2. Given group size and staffing restrictions, is teacher-organized small group time possible in your program? What other factors would you need to consider before implementing teacher-organized small groups? How else might you manage to accommodate small group activities in your program?

3. Why did Ms. Freeman decide to conduct the math games during teacher-organized small group time? How did children's prior knowledge affect this decision?

4. What activities would you plan for the other groups of children—those who are not participating in the teacher-organized small group?

7

Integration in Center Time

This chapter, focusing on center time, continues to emphasize the integration and coordination of learning opportunities. Center time—often referred to as "choice time"—should be at least 55 to 60 minutes long. During this period, children can choose to engage in a variety of activities in different areas within the classroom. These typically include centers for block play, dramatic play, water play, books, puzzles and math manipulatives, science-related items, and writing and art materials. Children can play by themselves in the various areas, or in small groups of their own making (though, for practicality, a limit on how many children may gather at one time in a single center might be set by the teacher).

Many learning opportunities arise spontaneously as the children play with and explore the equipment and materials available in the centers. Others are created when a teacher provides specific materials and suggestions during center time so children can further explore topics in which they have expressed prior interest.

Still other center time experiences are planned by the teacher as a part of an integrated curriculum to follow up on teacher-led activities implemented in another part of the school day (e.g., story time, circle time, or teacher-led small group time). These planned follow-up experiences are similar in some

ways to teacher-organized small group activities that build on story time or whole group circle time experiences. In both instances, the teacher-planned activity integrates with and extends a prior activity that took place in whole group time.

But there are differences, too. In small group time, only one activity is typically offered to the children, and the teacher directly guides children's engagement. In contrast, follow-up activities in center time are optional, and are among many choices available to the children. Children who choose to engage in the follow-up activities take the lead, instead of the teacher, though teachers may engage with children during these activities to support and guide their learning. If, during center time, children take an activity in an unanticipated direction, however, the teacher should honor their ideas and let them develop their ideas as they will.

Teachers are actively involved during center time, but they do not use center time for formal instruction. Instead, teachers follow the children's leads and respond in supportive ways to their choices. This approach—child-initiated play with responsive teacher support—has a long tradition in preschool education, and research has linked teachers' verbal engagement with children during center time to children's later language and literacy development. One group of researchers found links between teacher-child talk during preschool center time and children's language understanding in kindergarten. Specifically, they found that a higher level of language understanding in children was related to a higher frequency of teacher-child conversation, especially when the topics of the conversations were substantive and related to the activity at hand. They also found connections between high-quality teacher-child talk during preschool choice time and children's reading comprehension in fourth grade (Dickinson & Porche 2005).

Although center time cannot support the entire range of preschool learning by itself, it is nevertheless an important, unique learning context. In the research by Dickinson and Porche (2005), for example, the link found between the preschool experience and fourth grade reading achievement was the strongest when preschool instruction featured both high-quality, one-to-one talk between teacher and child during choice time *and* high-quality large group experiences focused on specific content. This research, along with other studies (e.g., Crain-Thoreson & Dale 1992; Senechal & LeFevre 2002; Justice et al. 2003), suggests that learning is increased when teachers utilize a variety of instructional contexts and when they link experiences provided in one context to related experiences in other contexts.

Logistics of center time

During center time, teachers move around the classroom interacting with children to support their work and play. Often, one of two teachers is designated as a "floater" and the other is stationed in an area that requires more constant adult support. The floater moves around the entire classroom, supporting the flow of activity and addressing

---

Box 7.1

Meaningful interaction during center time

As Michelle finishes painting at the easel, she calls Ms. Freeman over to look at her painting. The painting consists of many patches of color, scattered all over the large piece of paper. Two possible teacher responses are described here. Notice how much more meaningful the interaction is in the second example, where Ms. Freeman uses descriptive statements, open-ended comments, and active listening.

Response one

Ms. Freeman: What colors did you paint?

Michelle: [Points to each color in turn] Red, blue, red, green, yellow . . .

Ms. Freeman: Good job! You know all of your colors. Can you count all of the patches of colors to see how many you painted?

Michelle: [Points to the patches] 1, 2, 3, 4, 5, 6, 7, 8, 9.

Ms. Freeman: [Points to a patch that Michelle missed] I think you forgot to count this one. So you have . . .

Michelle: . . . 10.

Ms. Freeman: Good job! You know how to count, and you know all of your colors. Why don't you write your name on your painting, and hang it up to dry so everyone can see it.

Response two

Ms. Freeman: That's a very colorful painting. You worked on it a long time. Tell me about it.

Michelle: [Points to various patches as she talks] I made this one first. And then I made this one. I made this color when I mixed different colors. I started with yellow and then put blue in it. It's kind of green.

Ms. Freeman: Yes, I can see both yellow and blue streaks here. And then, right here in the middle, it's all green. How did you make it all green?

Michelle: I mixed and mixed and mixed them up, and they turned into green.

Increasing the Power of Instruction

children's specific concerns or questions. The teacher stationed in one area also keeps an eye on nearby centers. Of course, the dynamic nature of center time requires the teachers to communicate with each other and to adjust their movements and roles as needed.

Ideally, over the course of several weeks, all of the children participate in a fairly full range of center time activities. To encourage this, teachers gently guide and encourage children to extend their interests—from perhaps a couple of favorite centers early in the year to all, or at least most, centers by about the middle of the preschool year. Some of this gentle guidance is embedded in teachers' brief introductions to centers during whole group time. While in the whole group, children may make their first choices for center time. However, in the shorter term (within the framework of activities provided for one week, for example) children's engagement with every center activity is not at all necessary. Making children engage in all center time activities is inconsistent with the hallmark of center time—respecting children's choice and initiative. Some common approaches to facilitating center time use activity boards and signs with posted limits and sign-up sheets.

Activity boards

Some teachers use an activity board to facilitate center time. On the board, children can put their nametags in pockets under labeled pictures of each center. The number of pockets should match the maximum number of children that each center can accommodate at one time. As pockets are filled, children can see which areas still have room for more children. Children return to the activity board to move their nametags when they change areas. If all of the pockets for some activity areas are full, children know to select another area, and to check later to see whether there is an opening.

Teachers can be strategic when asking children to make their first choices, sometimes making suggestions that may put certain children together in order to support social relationships, or encouraging children with strong preferences

for just a few centers to broaden their interests. For example, near the beginning of the year, a teacher might let a shy child be among the first to choose to allow the child to make a choice uninfluenced by the number of children who will eventually be at that center. Or, a teacher might call on a child who tends to stick to certain favorite centers to choose last, so if her favorites are full by the time she gets to choose, she will have to try something new.

Using activity boards with children supports the integration of literacy, math, and language: Pictures of each center are labeled with print, and exposure to print helps build literacy skills. Children must use a math strategy (one-to-one matching) to compare the quantities of two sets; that is, how many pockets, how many nametags. Children also use math as they interpret a graphical representation of number (labeled pictures, with pockets underneath) and analyze that information (the number of full and empty pockets) to determine whether space is available. Language skills are supported, too, as children often engage in interesting conversations and problem solving when they return to the activity board to make a new choice. These conversations are particularly interesting when two children go together to choose a center that will accommodate both of them. With experience, they begin to consider both children's preferences, their mutual desire to play together, and the number of spaces available in the various centers, using the language-dependent social skills of negotiation and compromise.

Posted limits and sign-up lists

At the end of an introduction to center time, when each center is listed out loud, teachers can ask children to raise their hands when the center they wish to try first is mentioned. If too many children want to go to the same center, teachers can choose children to go first, and put the remaining children's names on a list. When a space opens, the next child on the list may join the center.

In addition, teachers can post signs in the individual centers indicating the maximum number of spaces each center allows. The signs indicate this maximum with both a numeral and a pictorial representation—such as faces—of the number. The signs provide physical support for the social expectation that the children will abide by class rules, and they also prompt children to engage in number-related problem solving. Children soon learn the limits for each area, and begin to count up from the number of children already there to the number allowed.

For example, a child approaching the block area might think: "There can only be four in the block area. Is there space for me and Sam? Keisha and Rashid are already there, that's two . . . Sam makes three . . . and I'm number four. Yes! We can both go in!" If there isn't room for both children, then the teacher can help them discuss other centers where they both can play. Or, children may think of strategies, such as one child entering the block area and using the last spot with the hope that another space will open soon so the second child can join.

Teachers can also post a sign-up sheet on a clipboard in each center. During center time, whenever a center is full, children may sign their names, in whatever way they are able, on this "turns" list. The teacher may wish to print the child's name next to the child's own writing on the sign-up sheet. When children leave the area, the next child on the list may enter, if he or she wishes. (By this point, the children who are waiting should have joined another center.) A teacher or the child who is leaving the center to pursue a new activity notifies the next child on the list. If this child is no longer interested, the next child on the list may enter the area.

A sign-up sheet provides a means for regulating spaces, gives children an opportunity to write their names for a purpose, and involves some thinking about number, such as when a child counts the names on the list above his or her own name. Children may also begin to recognize other children's names on the list.

When not enough spaces open up during a day's center time to accommodate every child wanting a turn in that area, the sign-up sheet is carried over to the next day. When introducing center time the following day, the teacher first asks children from the previous day's lists if they would like to start out in the area they had signed up for the day before.

Supporting children's learning as situations arise spontaneously

The children gathered in the dramatic play area of Ms. Freeman's classroom have negotiated a play scenario. A child holding a doll spontaneously announces, "It's my baby's birthday. Let's have a party." All the children gathered in the area agree. The children prepare invitations, consult directions on the back of an empty cake mix box, stir imaginary batter in a bowl, pour the "batter" into each cavity of a muffin tin, spin the numbered dial on the play oven, and arrange place settings on the table.

One child, Sarah, takes four small sheets of paper from the nearby writing center, folds each in half, and makes invitations to the party. She uses scribble writing and pictures, rather than real words, on the first three invitations. Sarah decorates the front of the fourth invitation—which she takes extra time making, since it is for her best friend—with a cupcake and candles. She decides not to use scribble writing on this important invitation, and asks Ms. Freeman for help spelling *please* and *come*. She considers the time of the party as well, stipulating that her friend should come at twelve o'clock. Sarah works hard to regulate the size of each of her letters

and is pleased to see that they are all approximately the same height.

Ms. Freeman calculates carefully her help with Sarah's spelling, basing it on her observations of this 4-year-old's current knowledge and skills. Ms. Freeman sounds out the phonemes in *please*, drawing out each as Sarah writes the corresponding letters. Ms. Freeman advises Sarah to add an *a* after the *e* in *please*, explaining that the word's middle sound is spelled with two letters rather than with *e* alone. She also explains that there is an *e* at the end of *please*, and indicates that Sarah can add *e* there, too. Using the same strategy, she helps the child write *come*.

Luis, who is also preparing for the birthday party, pauses as he distributes imaginary cupcakes to plates arranged on the table. "Do we have enough?" he asks himself. He jabs his finger into each of the muffin tin cavities, counting imaginary cupcakes: "1, 2, 3, 4, 5, 6." Then he walks around the table to count the plates: "1, 2, 3, 4, 5, 6, 7." As he is counting, Ms. Freeman notices that he counts a few plates twice. She says,

> I think you forgot where you started, and counted some plates more than once. I'll stand at this chair to remind you where you started, if you'd like to count the plates again.

With the teacher's support, Luis counts the five plates accurately.

Ms. Freeman reminds Luis that he had counted six cupcakes in the muffin tin. He asks, "Is that enough?" His question demonstrates a typical preschool understanding of number—children can recite the first five or even ten number words accurately, but they may not yet comprehend that number words coming later in the sequence represent larger quantities than number words coming earlier. To Luis's question, Ms. Freeman responds, "I wonder if there's a way you can find out?" Luis looks at her and shrugs. Though he wants to know the answer to his question, he doesn't know how to proceed. Sensing this, Ms. Freeman offers a suggestion:

> Maybe we can find some small blocks and you can put one little block in each spot in the muffin tin,

and we'll pretend they are cupcakes. Then, you can put one block on each plate to see if you have enough. Would you like to try that?"

Luis would, and he starts to gather blocks.

Preschool children need to draw upon a range of knowledge and skills in the course of their ongoing activities, just like adults do. At times, observant teachers respond to extend children's learning in ways that are consistent with the child's goals. In the above examples, Ms. Freeman offered timely advice and support tailored to the situations at hand. Depending on the situation, her involvement extended the children's knowledge, provided analytic information about print and speech, and modeled a strategy. In each situation, she provided direct and explicit guidance. This guidance, however, was spontaneous and informal—it was not taken from or tightly related to a pre-planned and sequenced set of lessons isolated from a functional context, such as from a curriculum planning book (Schickedanz 2003). Neither was it commanding—Ms. Freeman made sure her guidance was optional, and presented it to the children as helpful suggestions.

In these examples, we saw children involved in integrating and consolidating their own learning as they engaged freely with materials during center time, with the teacher providing support to help children meet their own objectives. When the children began planning a birthday party, they engaged in several different activities spanning multiple learning domains. For example, Sarah not only used literacy skills but also used several math-related skills when she set to work making invitations. First, on her trip to the writing center, she took the exact number of sheets of paper she needed to make invitations for the four friends she intended to invite. She then folded each piece of paper in half to create cards, and she carefully drew a plate in the center of the front of one card, as well as a cupcake right in the middle of the plate. She drew upon her knowledge of number and quantity, geometry, and spatial relations as she put her skills to use in a way that mattered to her.

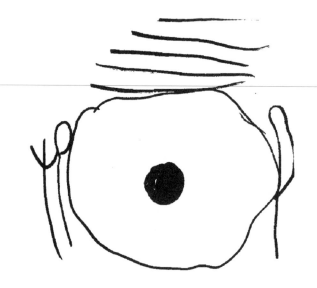

The literacy knowledge and skills Sarah used in this activity were acquired over weeks and months in other preschool contexts, as well as at home. She knew the names of letters and how letters are formed, she could link some speech sounds to letter names, and she knew that print is placed on a page from left to right. Later, when she set out to deliver her invitations, Sarah used language skills and social skills when she distributed them to her friends. To build upon this knowledge, Ms. Freeman provided literacy-related instruction—she segmented phonemes as she sounded out the words Sarah wished to spell. She also provided some additional suggestions regarding the spelling of *please* and *come*.

The other example of child-initiated learning within the birthday party activity—Luis's distribution of pretend cupcakes—was motivated by a social concern: Were there enough cupcakes for each guest? Ms. Freeman provided considerable scaffolding to help him answer this question. In Luis's activity, mathematics learning was the focus, although the teacher's engagement added exposure to more complex language, which benefits the child beyond the domain of mathematics. For example, she used several words referring to mental processes, such as *think*, *forgot*, *remind*, *wonder*, and *pretend*. Moreover, as is often the case when adults engage genuinely with children in conversation, she varied her syntax; at times it was fairly complex.

Ms. Freeman also proposed a three-step

mathematical plan for figuring out whether there would be enough cupcakes for each guest—a one-to-one correspondence task. The child needed first to find the small blocks, then put one block in each muffin tin cavity, and then place each block onto a plate. Although the teacher provided a fairly complex set of directions, Luis's prior knowledge, skill set, and high motivation, as well as the available props, allowed him to comprehend her suggestions quickly.

Supporting integration across learning domains

Many of the spontaneous learning opportunities that arise during center time integrate math, literacy, and language, as well as other curriculum domains. Often, a teacher's engagement with children as they play encourages such integration. Consider this example: Maria complains to Ms. Freeman that another child has used up all the long blocks, preventing her from finishing the house she is building. The teacher asks Maria to think about how she can use smaller blocks (of which there are plenty) to build the last part of her house. After a bit of experimentation, Maria figures out how to use some smaller blocks to span the same distance as one longer block.

In this example, we see the integration of learning across several subject domains as Maria grapples with this problem. First, the child uses language to explain the situation to Ms. Freeman and to understand her teacher's suggestion. Maria then tackles a mathematical problem that involves measurement, as she tries to figure out how to use several identical smaller blocks to span the distance needed to form a side of her house. She also engages in spatial problem solving when she discovers that a door can be made from several smaller blocks. This creation prompts her friend to rebuild one side of her house with a door of the same kind. To do this, she counts the number of smaller blocks Maria used, takes this number of blocks from the shelf, and rebuilds the wall of her own house.

With the houses now complete, Ms. Freeman thinks about how to integrate literacy skills into the children's play, as well. First, she comments on the design of the houses' doors and the children's use of the smaller blocks. Then, she tells the children, "It looks like this is a new neighborhood because there aren't any streets. I wonder if a street will be built to reach these houses?" The children decide that there does need to be a street, and they start building one immediately.

While the children do this, Ms. Freeman visits the writing center and cuts a piece of paper into small strips. Rashid, who is working at the writing center, asks what she is doing. Ms. Freeman explains that she is making street signs and invites Rashid to join her in playing street sign salespeople in the block area. He accepts. Together, they go to the block area and present themselves as salespeople. The two girls in the block area order several street signs, which the teacher and Rashid make by writing on paper strips and mounting the paper on Popsicle sticks with masking tape. They gather one-inch cube blocks and tape the free ends of the Popsicle sticks to the cubes, so the signs can stand up on street corners. Ms. Freeman lets the children leave their block buildings intact for use the next day, and she encourages them to make more signs when they return to the block area tomorrow.

Across days and even weeks, play of this kind can branch out in many directions, especially if children's constructions can be left up from one day to the next. The people living in the children's houses will need to receive mail, for example, which means that street addresses are needed. They will also need stores and other buildings, such as a post office and a library.

Teachers can also expand content knowledge, including vocabulary, as they talk with children and share information books with them to support their interest in building airports, train stations, farms, city neighborhoods, and so forth. Field trips also stimulate children's interest in these places, providing critical information and experiences that inform children's dramatic play.

Teachers can photograph children's block area creations to document their work and create further opportunities for language and literacy experiences. Children build language skills as they look at the pictures and talk about their buildings and play. Children can also use their literacy skills to help create captions for the photos. Looking at the photos, sorting them into groups for albums, and helping to compose and write the captions can be done during small group time. The teacher can serve as scribe for longer captions, but children can form letters and write out words for shorter ones. Finished albums can be placed in the library area. This activity illustrates how a coordinated series of learning experiences can begin in center time, move to small groups for follow-up, and then return to the center time context.

Supporting children's interest in math-related concepts

During center time, teachers can often help children pursue interests they have expressed or demonstrated. For example, after hearing a child talk about his new baby brother at snack time, a teacher might place books about new babies in the library corner, or add baby care props to the dramatic play center. Preschool teachers are quite accustomed to keeping their ears open for hints of children's interests—such as babies, airplanes, animals, or camping—and are usually quick to follow up with supportive materials.

However, they may be less likely to pick up on and follow up children's interests involving mathematics, and may be unsure of how to do so, even though such support can greatly benefit children. Let's look at two examples of a teacher following up on children's mathematical interests.

Exploring the concept of "one more"

At snack time, children help themselves to crackers from a basket. They are limited to six crackers each for their first helpings. A younger 3-year-old at the table places several crackers on her napkin, and Ms. Freeman helps her count them. There are five. Another child at the table, 5-year-old Sam, offers advice.

Sam: She needs one more.

Ms. Freeman: [Turns to toward the younger child] Why

don't you try that? Add one more cracker and then check to see how many you have.

Sam: I know how many, because six is right after five.

~~He helps the younger child count the crackers.~~

Sam: See! I knew it! I knew it! And if you put another cracker there, it would be seven, and then if you put *another* one, it would be eight.

The snack time conversation soon turns to something else, but Ms. Freeman keeps in mind Sam's interest in number. She wants to acknowledge his interest and encourage further development of his skill. So, during center time that same day, she informally explores the *one more* concept with a simple manipulatives-based game called Bears in a Cave (see Box 7.2).

Because of his interest in mathematics, Ms. Freeman thinks Sam will also be interested in the way Eric Carle's book *Rooster's Off to See the World* is organized. In this book, a rooster is joined in his travels by different groups of animals, each of which has one more animal in it than the last, up to a total of five. As the animals return home, the number of accompanying animals decreases, as one group at a time drops off in the reverse of the order in which they joined. Small pictures of the animals show how the groups increase and decrease as the story proceeds. Previously, Sam had demonstrated that he understood the concept of adding *one more,* and he was excited to learn more about it. This book goes one step further, though, and includes changes of *one less,* a concept Ms. Freeman is not sure he has considered.

Sam is enthusiastic about the book, and to further his interest in this math concept, Ms. Freeman creates related materials for him to explore. These materials consist of grids on a sheet of paper with rows of boxes ranging from one to ten, arranged similarly to the graphics in Carle's book. She also provides ten different stickers (including stars, balloons, colored circles, teddy bears, and smiley faces). This collection of stickers provides enough variety for Sam to fill the boxes in each row with a different sticker. If he wants to, he can increase the number of stickers in each row to show that each group of items is one bigger than the

---

Box 7.2

Let's play "Bears in a Cave"

Materials and games designed for children to use on their own make it possible for them to explore number relationships, as well as other math-related concepts and skills, without a teacher being continuously involved. One such game is Bears in a Cave (Nelson 1999), a partner game through which children explore part-part-whole relationships and are able to extend and consolidate their understanding as they play.

Before playing, the teacher explains how the game works: Using seven or eight counting bears (or other available objects) and a container to represent a cave, two children act out a scenario in which a group of bears decide to play hide-and-seek. While one child covers her eyes, the other child takes some of the bears and hides them in the "cave" by placing the container over them, leaving the remaining bears in plain sight. The child who has been covering her eyes looks at the remaining bears and tries to figure out how many bears are hiding in the cave.

This is highly motivating and challenging task for preschoolers, who tend to focus on the visible bears rather than the hidden ones.

Adapted from Copley (2000, 59).

---

last. The teacher provides enough grid sheets and stickers for other children, whose interests might be sparked by the materials, to participate. She provides the materials first during small group time, as one of two math activities from which children can choose; this also serves to further integrate curriculum between different learning contexts.

When Ms. Freeman first introduces the materials in small group time, she reminds Sam of their conversation at snack time. When using the grid materials, Sam and one of his friends are the only children in their small group of six who systematically use a unique kind of sticker in each column of the grid paper and who seem clearly to view the grid paper as a set of columns, increasing by one, from left to right. In contrast, the younger children in the group are intent on simply filling each little box with a sticker, and they fill their grids by rows, rather than progressing by vertical columns. Ms. Freeman anticipates this variety of uses. She knows that she can support and extend individual children's math learning, and that the same physical materials can provide different math experiences for children with a range of math skills. For example, when talking with a 3-year-old about the stickers the child has placed in one row of boxes, the teacher says, "Oh, you used several different kinds of stickers in this row, not stickers that were all alike. How many different kinds of stickers did you use here, in this row?"

After the activity is introduced during small group time, similar materials are made available for independent use during center time (that is, without the teacher's explicit instruction). In the manipulatives area, Ms. Freeman places laminated grids printed on heavy cardstock and a basket full of various small objects. Depending on their varying abilities, children use the grids and the accompanying objects to explore graphing, one-to-one matching (as they place one item in each grid box), and increments of *one more*, from one to ten (see illustration).

Exploring the meaning of "a few"

One day, as snack time is coming to an end, Ms. Freeman makes an announcement:

Ms. Freeman: Okay, children. As soon as each of you finishes your snack, I'm going to start sending you to your cubbies a few at a time, because it will take a long time to get dressed to go outside in the cold and snowy weather. Jason and Luis, why don't you go to your cubbies first, since you're done.

Ana: Does "a few" mean two?

Ms. Freeman: Sometimes, but not always. It depends. If there were twenty children, I might call a few of you up, and maybe that would be four children. "A few" just means some, not many.

The conversation continues for a while, with the teacher providing more information about terms such as *a couple, a few, some, half, most,* and *almost all.* Ana is quite interested in these words and in the idea that the number of items in the group determines how many items end up being *a few, most,* or *half.* Though interested, she seems puzzled by these words that refer to different quantities

depending on the context of their use.

Based on Ana's interest, Ms. Freeman decides to follow up on this learning experience during center time. She sits down with Ana, and together they sort the class's collection of shells in a number of different ways and talk about these groupings using quantitative words and phrases such as *a few, most, half, almost all,* and *all.* Two other children become intrigued, and after a few more minutes of modeling, Ms. Freeman moves aside so they can join Ana in playing with the shells.

Games

Simple card games, board games, games involving manipulatives, and the like, are also excellent center time choices to foster math learning (Baroody & Wilkins 1999; Williams, Cunningham, & Lubawy 2005; MacDonald 2007; Nelson 2007). After games have been introduced and played once or twice in a teacher-organized small group setting, game pieces and materials can be set out on shelves and children can choose to play with them during center time. For example, two children who both know the numbers one through ten can play the classic card game War, which develops skill in number recognition and quantity comparison (teachers may

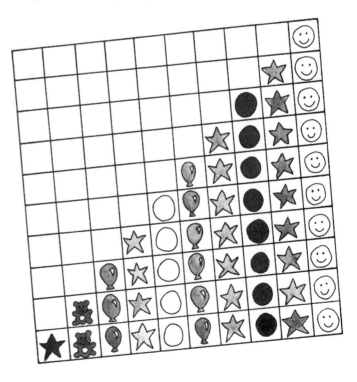

want to remove the face cards to simplify the game). Board games such as Parcheesi, Hi Ho! Cherry-O, and Chutes and Ladders teach social skills, such as taking turns, while also fostering basic number and operations skills as children move game pieces a specified number of places forward or backward on the board.

Games and activities involving manipulatives can be either purchased or made from a variety of materials. For example, a PVC pipe plumbing elbow with a drain can be used to teach addition, as children put marbles in from both sides and count how many come out (MacDonald 2007). Bears in a Cave (described earlier) is another manipulatives game that involves both math and dramatic play.

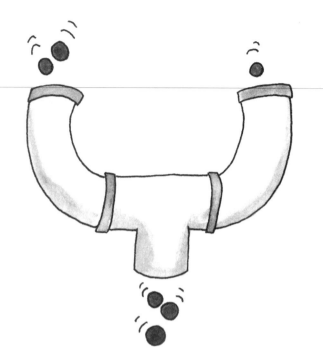

Following up on teacher-led activities in center time

In the vignette that begins this book, a child in the library corner, Jason, discovers a picture in a book of a lizard he recognizes from a story his teacher read to the class during story time. Now we can revisit that scenario as an example of following up on teacher-led activities during center time.

Over the last month, Ms. Freeman had exposed the children to a variety of animals in several books she had read to them (including *Rabbits and Raindrops*; *Raccoon on His Own*; *Hi, Harry*; *Over in the Meadow*; and *A Color of His Own*). To follow up on those story readings, Ms. Freeman places the book with the lizard picture in the class library, along with several other information books about reptiles and amphibians. When introducing center time that day, she tells the children about these books she has made available in the library corner, and draws some connections to the books that she has read aloud to the whole group on several occasions:

> I think you might find a picture of a lizard like the one we saw in *Raccoon on His Own*. If you are interested, you might want to look at the books about lizards, snakes, and turtles that I found for our library.

Follow-up activities in centers that relate to previous, teacher-led experiences can vary widely. (See Box 7.4 for some related to food and

cooking.) For example, in Chapter 4, there are two descriptions of follow-up activities to the reading of *One Duck Stuck*. One of these is a matching game that supports print-related learning. It uses animal pictures and the printed words for animal sounds. Ms. Freeman introduced the activity during whole group time, and then placed the materials in the puzzles and manipulatives center for children's independent use during center/choice time. The other follow-up activity for *One Duck Stuck* provides felt pieces and a felt board. After reading the book to the class three times, Ms. Freeman placed these materials in the library area for children to use to retell the story during center time.

◆　◆　◆

As the examples in this chapter have illustrated, center time provides a unique opportunity for children to choose from among several activities and take their play in unusual and creative directions. Center time provides children with opportunities to engage with other children—to make friends, share and negotiate ideas, and solve problems. This context also offers opportunities for integrating learning across various subject domains. While learning from different domains can be integrated within and across many other preschool settings,

Increasing the Power of Instruction

Box 7.4

Follow-up activities with food and cooking themes

At various times throughout the year, many preschool programs incorporate food and cooking topics into different learning contexts. For example, a class might explore measuring and the qualities of different ingredients as they bake a cake. Or, as part of a plant unit that includes a focus on plant-based foods, children might grow beans. Through field trips, children might even get to find out what life on a farm is like, how vegetable farms differ from dairy farms, and how both differ from fruit orchards.

These experiences can involve children in preparing food, reading food- or cooking-related storybooks, planting seeds, and more. Many of these types of activities are suitable for a small group context. Center time, then, is an excellent venue for following up on these experiences. Here are some ideas; in these examples, teachers may first need to provide props and explanations, but then should allow children full rein in the activity.

Making pretend cakes

Children can make pretend cakes out of blocks. One variation, which the teacher can demonstrate, is to place blocks inside shallow boxes to represent sheet cakes (small wooden cubes in note card boxes work well). In addition to fostering interaction between children as they pretend to share pieces of cake, this is an excellent setup for math learning as portions are divvied up.

To engage children in this activity, the teacher can refer to the children's previous experience of baking a real cake and dividing it for tasting. The teacher can also mention occasions featuring cakes, such as birthdays or weddings, which children might have experienced. The teacher might also remind children of relevant storybooks they have listened to, such as Karen Magnuson Beil's *A Cake All for Me* or B.G. Hennessy's *Jake Baked the Cake*. The teacher can suggest that children serve cake in the house area to their friends, perhaps in celebration of one of the doll's birthdays.

Using measuring cups and spoons at the water table

Often children have used measuring cups and spoons in cooking projects or have seen them used in books. The teacher can offer a variety of plastic measuring cups at the water table. This fosters hands-on exploration of measurement and of some common measurement tools used in cooking. The cups should vary in capacity, from one and two cups to one-half, one-third, and one-fourth of a cup. The teacher can also provide several sets of plastic measuring spoons.

If the classroom doesn't have one large water table, an alternate setup can be created on a regular table. A small tub of water can be set at each end of the table beside an additional container holding measuring cups and spoons. A few plastic bowls can be set up in the middle of the table, on top of an upside down container, which also divides the table into two play spaces. This setup can accommodate four children at a time—a pair at each end of the table. Each pair shares a tub of water and a box of measuring tools, and all four children use the bowls sitting on the container in the center of the table.

When introducing this activity, the teacher should remind children of how measuring implements are used when cooking. The teacher can suggest that the children try various things, such as measuring the water or pretending that they are mixing ingredients for cake batter.

Ingredient word matching

For this activity, the teacher makes word cards featuring the names of ingredients used in a recipe that the class has made or that have been used in a book the class has discussed (such as *A Cake All for Me*, Philemon Sturges's *The Little Red Hen (Makes Pizza)*, or Janet Stevens and Susan Stevens Crummel's *Cook-A-Doodle-Doo*).

For example, a cake might include milk, sugar, flour, vanilla, chocolate chips, salt, baking powder, and margarine. These words are printed on cards and laminated, a hole is punched in the upper left corner of each card, and the cards are secured together so that they won't become scattered and lost. If the words reflect the ingredients in a recipe from a particular book, the cards can be set out with that book on a large tray for exploration in the puzzles and manipulatives center. This center is a

Continued on the next page.

Continued from the previous page.

good choice for the activity because there is space to set out all the materials together.

This activity can be especially useful when reinforcing a previous book reading focused on food or cooking and when focusing children's attention on environmental print. The children find matches in the books for the words the teacher prints on the cards. In the books, the words are found on the labels of ingredient containers—an example of a real-world use of print. Typically, children interpret environmental print by "reading" the entire context, not primarily by looking at the print (Reutzel et al. 2003). The teacher can turn to a page in the book and read the name of an ingredient that appears in the text or illustrations. Relevant pages of the book can even be photocopied and laminated so that they can be left with the ingredient cards.

Because this activity requires some teacher modeling in order for children to understand it, the teacher probably should demonstrate it first during small group time and then make the materials available to children during center time.

The teacher might prepare a shopping list with cake ingredients and other words on it, and also recipe charts for cakes, muffins, and other foods. When engaging in dramatic play during center time, children can check the empty containers provided for house play to see if they have everything they need to pretend cook. If they need to purchase something, they can check the prepared list of shopping items (featuring ingredient words with accompanying pictures) to see if the item is there. If not, they can add it to the list in any way they wish and then pretend to go shopping. Other objects such as blocks can stand in for missing ingredients.

center/choice time allows for more integration of learning within a single activity or scenario than any other learning context.

Center time also encourages different patterns to emerge in the relationships between adults and children. To be sure, teachers are responsive to children and take their interests and understanding into account throughout all portions of the preschool day. But in most learning contexts, teachers take the lead. During center time, however, children lead;

this causes the adult-child relationship to change. Center time activities do far more than simply give children opportunities to make choices—they encourage leadership experiences. It is important to foster children's leadership skills early, in preschool, to lay the foundation for the skills and knowledge children will need in the future.

For all of these reasons, center time has long been, and should continue to be, the core of the preschool program.

Reflection questions

1. When implementing follow-up activities, when would you choose a center time context over a teacher-led small group context? What are the biggest differences between the two learning contexts?

2. Given that center time allows children to choose and direct their own activities, how can children be encouraged to try new things or engage with different people during this time?

3. How can teachers build on children's prior knowledge during center time? How can they work with children's interests? What were some of the ways that Ms. Freeman both supported children's interests *and* took their prior knowledge into consideration?

4. In what ways does center time offer unique integration opportunities?

Concluding Thoughts

I was inspired to write this book by preschool teachers and the particular challenges they face today. Teachers understand the need to include important content and skills in their programs, make their teaching intentional, enhance their explicit and teacher-guided instruction, and increase their engagement in responsive and supportive ways in both child-initiated and teacher-guided learning. At the same time, preschool teachers often feel that young children's learning has become too fragmented, that daily schedules are stretched beyond comfortable limits, and that core components of the preschool program, such as center time, are in danger of neglect. Integration is essential in addressing these problems.

Integrating learning in a meaningful way can be demanding. First, very careful and thoughtful planning is required to avoid undermining certain key goals in order to achieve others. Learning experiences need to be planned for the classroom contexts that best suit the teaching purposes, and they need to be integrated across the day for maximum effect. In addition, before integrating curriculum from two or more domains, teachers must have a strong grasp of each learning domain in its own right. Over the past ten years, much emphasis has been placed on specific learning areas within various curriculum domains, such as phonological awareness and inferential reasoning in literacy; and number, geometry and spatial relations, and measurement in mathematics.

In this book, my approach to integrating learning focuses on increasing the power of instruction. We must always focus on maximizing children's learning as we plan instructional experiences and work with children. Teachers might worry that a greater emphasis on instruction and learning will diminish children's social and emotional well-being and their development of social skills. As educators we must indeed ensure that the early childhood setting supports every aspect of children's learning and development, because all areas are important to their present and future well-being, and because social competence and the development of skills such as self-regulation are strong predictors of academic achievement (McClelland, Morrison, & Holmes 2000; Spira, Bracken, & Fischell 2005; Duncan et al. 2007).

As this book illustrates, part of our basic obligation to children involves balancing the content instruction and skill development we have planned with our responses to children as they engage with the learning experiences we provide. When instruction is balanced with feedback and conversations aimed at supporting a child's understanding—rather than fixated narrowly on what is or isn't "right"—we show children how much we value them (Hamre & Pianta 2001). We need to address children's confusion and genuinely try to understand and help them work through it (Schickedanz 2007).

We build relationships and bolster learning when a daily schedule is balanced to include a variety of roles for both children and adults, and when adults are supportive—but not intrusive—when it is children's turn to both choose and largely direct their activities. When teachers notice individual children's interests and follow up on those interests, it extends important skills and knowledge and shows children that we care. We also offer key support to children when we balance the kinds of groupings encountered throughout the day, as relationship opportunities differ across large group, small group, and individual contexts.

This book's hypothetical Ms. Freeman illustrated how an experienced teacher makes judgments when planning, preparing, and implementing instruction. As her example demonstrates, a considerable amount of discretion and decision making regarding instruction resides with the teacher. Teachers are the most important part of any learning context.

Preschool teachers are hard workers, committed to children, and interested in learning more about improving children's opportunities for learning. As this book has shown, strategic, carefully planned integration can increase children's overall learning in the limited preschool day. When more learning is included throughout the day, and when more activities are followed up—both within and across learning contexts—children's learning is deepened. Integration can decrease fragmentation and isolation of learning, aiding comprehension and ultimately making learning more meaningful.

When our efforts achieve these teaching and learning goals, we know we are making a difference in the lives of children.

Appendices

Appendix A

Math-Related Children's Books

There are many excellent children's books with math-related themes and content. We have selected some examples here, organized by the standards of the National Council of Teachers of Mathematics. These standards are

- number and operations;
- patterns and algebra;
- geometry and spatial relations;
- measurement; and
- data analysis and probability (NCTM 2000).

These books also feature rich vocabulary important for both captivating young children's imaginations and building their language skills. A few selections are either wordless or with sparse text, instead featuring outstanding illustrations that teachers can discuss with children.

Consider enriching your preschool library with these wonderful choices, which are sure to delight preschoolers ages 3–5. Many of these books can be checked out of your local library or bought used in bookstores or online.

Number and operations

Aker, S. Illustrated by B. Karlin. *What comes in 2's, 3's, & 4's?*

This book invites children to count various objects that are grouped in small amounts. Rich math vocabulary reinforces concepts familiar to young children.

Baker, K. *Big fat hen.*

A hen lays eggs in quantities that increase by two, up to a total of ten. This book features number comparison, object grouping, addition, and subtraction.

Baker, K. *Quack and count.*

Using simple verse with rhymes and alliteration, this book teaches children about the different ways numbers can be added together to equal seven. Through illustrations of varying numbers of ducklings (which children can find on each page and count), children learn about different ways to add to get the same result.

Bang, M. *Ten, nine, eight.*

Each page focuses on a set of objects found in a young girl's bedroom, on her clothing, or on her body. The number of objects featured diminishes by one on each successive page. Shapes of objects (e.g., round buttons) and the objects' locations (e.g., hanging down) are sometimes noted in the text. [also in Geometry and Spatial Relations]

Capucilli, A. Illustrated by J. Rankin. *Mrs. McTats and her houseful of cats.*

Mrs. McTats welcomes cats into her home, often in multiples, until she has a total of 25. Using good math vocabulary, this book encourages young children to think about adding more than one item at a time.

Carle, E. *Rooster's off to see the world.*

A rooster, on a walk to see the world, is joined one at a time by other animals. But when it begins to get dark, animals leave one by one to return home. Both increases and decreases by one are depicted in a graph on each page. (For suggestions on using this book during center time, see Chapter 7.)

Carter, D.A. *How many bugs in a box?*
[see Measurement]

Coxe, M. *6 sticks.*

Six Popsicle sticks are rearranged to make many different objects, which appear in subsets (e.g. two skis each for three people). The sparse text names the number of sticks (always six) and how many of each creation there are (e.g., three *t*s). Children can count the sticks in each illustration, realizing that the same total is reached each time.
[also in Geometry and Spatial Relations]

Fox, M. Illustrated by P. Mullins. *Hattie and the fox.*

Hattie the hen notices something in the bushes—a fox—and announces to the other barnyard animals the body parts she detects. This story introduces the concept of "parts of a whole"—that creatures and objects can be broken down into smaller parts.
[also in Data Analysis and Probability]

Giganti, P. Illustrated by D. Crews. *Each orange has 8 slices: A counting book.*

Each illustrated spread depicts a number of items and some of their parts, such as "2 calves" with "4 skinny legs" each, followed by prompts to count them. This book provides pictorial representation of numbers and groupings (e.g., three tricycles with three wheels each; two clowns, each holding two bunches of five balloons).
[also in Data Analysis and Probability]

Lee, H.V. *1, 2, 3, Go!*

This number concept book shows children playing actively (e.g., catching a butterfly, hitting drums). The number of children depicted on each successive page increases by one, up to a total of ten. Chinese characters, appearing in the right margin, add to the scope of the book.

Leuck, L. Illustrated by C. Vulliamy. *My baby brother has ten tiny toes.*

In rhyming verse rich in alliteration, a big sister names her baby brother's body parts, toys, clothing, and eating utensils. The number of each item progresses from one to ten. Pictures invite children to locate and count the objects featured on each page.

London, J. Illustrated by M. Moore. *Count the ways, little brown bear.*

Mother Bear compares her love for Little Bear to Little Bear's fondness for various things, with examples progressing from one to ten. Groupings of objects sometimes show subsets. This book includes ideas of comparing and contrasting, counting, and number grouping.

Moss, L. Illustrated by M. Priceman. *Zin! Zin! Zin! A violin.*

Orchestral instruments are introduced one by one in verse, with each one joining its sounds with those already introduced. This book reinforces counting skills and the addition of one to a group of similar objects. It also details the kind of sounds each instrument makes.

Stevens, J., & S.S. Crummel. *Cook-a-doodle-doo!*
[see Measurement]

Wallwork, A. *No dodos: A counting book of endangered animals.*
[see Patterns and Algebra]

Wellington, M. *Mr. Cookie Baker.*
[see Measurement]

Patterns and algebra

Grossman, V. Illustrated by S. Long. *Ten little rabbits.*

Ten rabbits wear Native American blankets from five different tribes. The patterns woven into the blankets are intricately colored, and each blanket is labeled with the name of its corresponding tribe and information about the tribe's cultural traditions. The blankets can serve as a discussion starter on the topic of patterns.

Paul, A.W. Illustrated by J. Winter. *Eight hands round: A patchwork alphabet.*

Patchwork quilt patterns are illustrated, labeled, and described in this book. Twenty-six patterns—one for each letter of the alphabet—are pictured and accompanied by written descriptions of the patterns.

Pinkney, B. *Max found two sticks.*

After he realizes that rhythm is everywhere in his environment, Max uses two sticks that he finds outside to make his own beats. Drumming on different objects, he imitates the sounds and patterns of his neighborhood. Children will enjoy hearing and repeating the words representing Max's rhythms and sounds.

Rotner, S., & R. Olivo. *Close, closer, closest.*

Enlarged photographs show what objects look like from three different distances: close, closer, and closest. Children can learn about the patterns that make up familiar objects. Children are also exposed to three-dimensional shapes and textures.

Stockdale, S. *Nature's paintbrush: The patterns and colors around you.*

This book shows children that in nature, colors and patterns are all around us. Examples include the tiger, which uses his stripes to hide in the grass, and the cactus, which has patterned spines to protect it from predators. Children can learn to spot patterns as well as things that interrupt patterns.

Wallwork, A. *No dodos: A counting book of endangered animals.*

This counting book also contains themes of patterns and algebra. Each page uses shape and color to create patterned borders, a technique that children can copy and use in their own work. [also in Number and Operations]

Geometry and spatial relations

Ayers, K. Illustrated by N.B. Westcott. *Up, down, and around.*

Through verse, this book contrasts plants that grow down (e.g., carrots), up (e.g., corn), and around (e.g., tomato vines). Engaging pictures help children think about different types of spaces and directions.

Bang, M. *Ten, nine, eight.*
[see Number and Operations]

Baranski, J. Illustrated by Y.M. Han. *Round is a pancake.*

Rhyming verse filled with alliteration names things that are round, all of which are depicted in lively illustrations. On the last few pages, complex scenes filled with different items encourage children to search for additional round objects.

Coxe, M. *6 sticks.*
[see Number and Operations]

Dodds, D. Illustrated by J. Lacome. *The shape of things.*

This patterned rhyming text first presents a flat shape (e.g., a square) and then adds other elements to create familiar objects out of that shape (e.g., a house). After learning about many different shapes, children can apply this knowledge in the final spread by finding examples of shapes in new locations.

Ehlert, L. *Color zoo.*

The pictures in this book use geometric shapes to form animals. Children can identify the shapes used to compose each animal. The pages of the book are cut out in shapes, as well.

Hutchins, P. *Changes, changes.*

This wordless picture book portrays two characters as they arrange and rearrange the same set of colored blocks to create different shapes and objects. Children can interpret the scenes and fill in the story as they see how the same set of blocks can be used to make many different things.

Hutchins, P. *Rosie's walk.*

Rosie the hen goes for a walk around the farmyard, not realizing a fox is following her. Rich spatial vocabulary is featured as the fox tries to keep up with Rosie on her winding route.

Leake, D. *Finding shapes: Rectangles.*

Rectangles are described using geometry-related vocabulary. Children are invited to find rectangles in many common objects. (Part of a set of four books; the others feature circles, triangles, and squares.)

Peat, A. *Shapes.*

The features of shapes are explained, compared, and contrasted through colorful diagrams and simple text. Photographs of objects encourage children to find shapes in the environment.

Skalak, B. Illustrated by S. Long. *Waddle, waddle, quack, quack, quack.*

Five ducklings hatch from five eggs and set out with their mother to explore the world. One duckling, though, gets lost. The rhyming verse is rich in spatial terms as the ducklings move about and the lost duckling searches for his family.

Stockdale, S. *Carry me: Animal babies on the move.*

This information book shows a variety of mother animals carrying their babies. Some are carried on the mother's back, others are carried in the mother's teeth, while still others are held in the mother's arms. Children learn about spatial relationships from these different mother-child interactions.

Thong, R. Illustrated by G. Lin. *Round is a mooncake.*

A book of verse in which round, square, and rectangular things are located within a variety of environmental contexts. On several pages, children are invited to find shapes in objects that have not been discussed.

Measurement

Allen, P. *Who sank the boat?*

Animals attempt to balance their weight in a boat, but unfortunately, the boat sinks. This book introduces weight and balance experiences, which children can experiment with at the classroom water table.

Carter, D.A. *How many bugs in a box?*

Providing an introduction to the concept of capacity, this pop-up counting book features a variety of boxes, each holding a specific number of bugs. [also in Number and Operations]

Leedy, L. *Tracks in the sand.*

This story of the life cycle of a sea turtle features vocabulary used to measure time (such as *full moon, night, day, season,* and *years*).

Miller, M. *Now I'm big.*

Filled with photographs of babies and 3- and 4-year-olds, this book talks about what children can do now that they are "big." This can be used to prompt discussions related to growth and measurement.

Say, A. *The bicycle man.*

Japanese children holding a sports festival in their country schoolyard are charmed by the bicycle tricks of an American soldier. This story incorporates measurement skills in the context of judging sports events.

Stevens, J., & S.S. Crummel. *Cook-a-doodle-doo!*

A rooster enlists the help of a turtle, a pig, and an iguana in making strawberry shortcake. Through humorous interpretations of ingredients and measuring devices, which ultimately reinforce the correct meanings of items such as teaspoons, children learn about measurement. [also in Number and Operations]

Tompert, A. Illustrated by L.M. Munsinger. *Just a little bit.*

This story, about a mouse and an elephant playing on a seesaw, uses illustrations and text that encourages young children to think about measurement.

Wellington, M. *Mr. Cookie Baker.*

A baker locates and measures the ingredients he needs to make cookies. Bright illustrations show utensils, measuring cups and spoons, and a kitchen timer. Varying amounts of cookies are shown on trays, and flat pieces of dough are shown with holes left by cookies cut out of them. [also in Number and Operations]

Data analysis and probability

Baker, A. *Gray rabbit's odd one out.*

Each page features a particular category (e.g., animals), but one item on each page does not fit (e.g., not an animal). Children learn about object analysis and the process of elimination.

Fox, M. Illustrated by P. Mullins. *Hattie and the fox.* [see Number and Operations]

George, L.B. *In the garden: Who's been here?*

In this information book, two children visit their garden to pick vegetables for their mother. While there, they notice clues indicating the presence of animals. Children can join in trying to find clues and figuring out which animals might have left them. (One in the *Who's Been Here?* series of books.)

Giganti, P. Illustrated by D. Crews. *Each orange has 8 slices: A counting book.* [see Number and Operations]

Hindley, J. Illustrated by I. Bates. *Do like a duck does.*

A fox, pretending to be a duck, joins a mother duck and her five ducklings. Suspicious, the mother names the features of ducks and contrasts these with the fox's. This book encourages the discussion of categories and classification.

Jenkins, S., & R. Page. *What do you do with a tail like this?*

This book, about the body parts of different animals, shows one part on each spread, along with a question: "What do you do with a tail (or nose, mouth, etc.) like this?" The book provides partial data, in a guessing/thinking format, and then shows full data to support children's analysis.

Morris, A. *Shoes shoes shoes.*

Shoes are loosely organized into categories such as working shoes, dancing shoes, shoes for ice or snow, and anytime-at-all shoes. Children can learn that objects of almost any type can be divided into groups based on common attributes.

Onishi, S. *Who's hiding?*

This book features eighteen animals, which are always pictured in the same order in three rows of six. All of the animals are shown on the first page, but one of the animals is hiding on some of the pages—only one feature, not its whole body, is visible. Children must analyze the illustrations to determine which animal is hiding. On other pages, one animal differs from the others in one way—e.g., is crying, is sleeping, has horns, etc.

Appendix B

Mathematics Expectations for Prekindergarten Through Second Grade

From: NCTM's Principles and Standards for School Mathematics

Number and operations standard

Instructional programs from pre-kindergarten through grade 12 should enable all students to—	**Expectations for grades pre-K–2** *In prekindergarten through grade 2 all students should—*
Understand numbers, ways of representing numbers, relationships among numbers, and number systems	• count with understanding and recognize "how many" in sets of objects • use multiple models to develop initial understandings of place value and the base-ten number system • develop understanding of the relative position and magnitude of whole numbers and of ordinal and cardinal numbers and their connections • develop a sense of whole numbers and represent and use them in flexible ways, including relating, composing, and decomposing numbers • connect number words and numerals to the quantities they represent, using various physical models and representations • understand and represent commonly used fractions, such as ¼, , and ½
Understand meanings of operations and how they relate to one another	• understand various meanings of addition and subtraction of whole numbers and the relationship between the two operations • understand the effects of adding and subtracting whole numbers • understand situations that entail multiplication and division, such as equal groupings of objects and sharing equally
Compute fluently and make reasonable estimates	• develop and use strategies for whole-number computations, with a focus on addition and subtraction • develop fluency with basic number combinations for addition and subtraction • use a variety of methods and tools to compute, including objects, mental computation, estimation, paper and pencil, and calculators

Note: The full text of these principles and standards for pre-K–2, with examples and guidance for instruction, is available online at www.nctm.org. *Source:* Reprinted, by permission, from National Council of Teachers of Mathematics, "Standards for Grades Pre-K–2," *Principles and Standards for School Mathematics* (Reston, VA: NCTM, 2000), 78, 90, 96, 102.

Increasing the Power of Instruction

[Patterns, functions, and] algebra standard

Instructional programs from pre-kindergarten through grade 12 should enable all students to—	Expectations for grades pre-K–2 *In prekindergarten through grade 2 all students should—*
Understand patterns, relations, and functions	• sort, classify, and order objects by size, number, and other properties • recognize, describe, and extend patterns such as sequences of sounds and shapes or simple numeric patterns and translate from one representation to another • analyze how both repeating and growing patterns are generated
Represent and analyze mathematical situations and structures using algebraic symbols	• illustrate general principles and properties of operations, such as commutativity, using specific numbers • use concrete, pictorial, and verbal representations to develop an understanding of invented and conventional symbolic notations
Use mathematical models to represent and understand quantitative relationships	• model situations that involve the addition and subtraction of whole numbers, using objects, pictures, and symbols
Analyze change in various contexts	• describe qualitative change, such as a student's growing taller; describe quantitative change, such as a student's growing two inches in one year

Geometry standard

Instructional programs from pre-kindergarten through grade 12 should enable all students to—	Expectations for grades pre-K–2 *In prekindergarten through grade 2 all students should—*
Analyze characteristics and properties of two- and three-dimensional geometric shapes and develop mathematical arguments about geometric relationships	• recognize, name, build, draw, compare, and sort two- and three-dimensional shapes • describe attributes and parts of two- and three-dimensional shapes • investigate and predict the results of putting together and taking apart two- and three-dimensional shapes
Specify locations and describe spatial relationships using coordinate geometry and other representational systems	• describe, name, and interpret relative positions in space and apply ideas about relative position • describe, name, and interpret direction and distance in navigating space and apply ideas about direction and distance • find and name locations with simple relationships such as "near to" and in coordinate systems such as maps
Apply transformations and use symmetry to analyze mathematical situations	• recognize and apply slides, flips, and turns • recognize and create shapes that have symmetry
Use visualization, spatial reasoning, and geometric modeling to solve problems	• create mental images of geometric shapes using spatial memory and spatial visualization • recognize and represent shapes from different perspectives • relate ideas in geometry to ideas in number and measurement • recognize geometric shapes and structures in the environment and specify their location

Measurement standard

Instructional programs from pre-kindergarten through grade 12 should enable all students to—	Expectations for grades pre-K–2 *In prekindergarten through grade 2 all students should—*
Understand measurable attributes of objects and the units, systems, and processes of measurement	• recognize the attributes of length, volume, weight, area, and time • compare and order objects according to these attributes • understand how to measure using nonstandard and standard units • select an appropriate unit and tool for the attribute being measured
Apply appropriate techniques, tools, and formulas to determine measurements	• measure with multiple copies of units of the same size, such as paper clips laid end to end • use repetition of a single unit to measure something larger than the unit, for instance, measuring the length of a room with a single meterstick • use tools to measure • develop common referents for measures to make comparisons and estimates

Data analysis and probability standard

Instructional programs from pre-kindergarten through grade 12 should enable all students to—	Expectations for grades pre-K–2 *In prekindergarten through grade 2 all students should—*
Formulate questions that can be addressed with data and collect, organize, and display relevant data to answer them	• pose questions and gather data about themselves and their surroundings • sort and classify objects according to their attributes and organize data about the objects • represent data using concrete objects, pictures, and graphs
Select and use appropriate statistical methods to analyze data	• describe parts of the data and the set of data as a whole to determine what the data show
Develop and evaluate inferences and predictions that are based on data	• discuss events related to students' experiences as likely or unlikely
Understand and apply basic concepts of probability	

Appendix C

Learning PATHS and Teaching STRATEGIES in Early Mathematics

From: Early Childhood Mathematics: Promoting Good Beginnings. A joint position statement of the
National Association for the Education of Young Children and the National Council of Teachers of Mathematics

The research base for sketching a picture of children's mathematical development varies considerably from one area of mathematics to another. Outlining a learning path, moreover, does not mean we can predict with confidence where a child of a given age will be in that sequence. Developmental variation is the norm, not the exception. However, children do tend to follow similar *sequences,* or *learning paths,* as they develop. This chart illustrates in each area some things that *many* children know and do—early and late in the three-to-six age range. These are, then, simply two points along the learning path that may have many steps in between. For each content area, the Sample Teaching Strategies column shows a few of the many teacher actions that promote learning when used within a classroom context that reflects the recommendations set forth in the NAEYC/NCTM position statement. In general, they are helpful strategies, with minor adaptations, across the age range.

Content Area	Examples of Typical Knowledge and Skills From Age 3 ⟶ Age 6		Sample Teaching Strategies
Number and operations	Counts a collection of one to four items and begins to understand that the last counting word tells *how many.*	Counts and produces (counts out) collections up to 100 using groups of 10.	Models counting of small collections and guides children's counting in everyday situations, emphasizing that we use one counting word for each object: ♡ ♡ ♡ "One…two…three…" Models counting by 10s while making groups of 10s (e.g., 10, 20, 30…or 14, 24, 34…).
	Quickly "sees" and labels collections of one to three with a number.	Quickly "sees" and labels with the correct number "patterned" collections (e.g., dominoes) and unpatterned collections of up to about six items.	Gives children a brief glimpse (a couple of seconds) of a small collection of items and asks how many there are.

Content Area	Examples of Typical Knowledge and Skills From Age 3 ————————→ Age 6		Sample Teaching Strategies
Number and operations	Adds and subtracts non-verbally when numbers are very low. For example, when one ball and then another are put into the box, expects the box to contain two balls.	Adds or subtracts using counting-based strategies such as counting on (e.g., adding 3 to 5, says "Five..., six, seven, eight"), when numbers and totals do not go beyond 10.	Tells real-life stories involving numbers and a problem. Asks *how many* questions (e.g., how many are left? how many are there now? how many did they start with? how many were added?). Shows children the use of objects, fingers, counting on, guessing, and checking to solve problems.
Geometry and spatial sense	Begins to match and name 2-D and 3-D shapes, first only with same size and orientation, then shapes that differ in size and orientation (e.g., a large triangle sitting on its point versus a small one sitting on its side).	Recognizes and names a variety of 2-D and 3-D shapes (e.g., quadrilaterals, trapezoids, rhombi, hexagons, spheres, cubes) in any orientation. Describes basic features of shapes (e.g., number of sides or angles).	Introduces and labels a wide variety of shapes (e.g., skinny triangles, fat rectangles, prisms) that are in a variety of positions (e.g., a square or a triangle standing on a corner, a cylinder "standing up" or horizontal). Involves children in constructing shapes and talking about their features.
	Uses shapes, separately, to create a picture. Describes object locations with spatial words such as *under* and *behind* and builds simple but meaningful "maps" with toys such as houses, cars, and trees.	Makes a picture by combining shapes. Builds, draws, or follows simple maps of familiar places, such as the classroom or playground.	Encourages children to make pictures or models of familiar objects using shape blocks, paper shapes, or other materials. Encourages children to make and talk about models with blocks and toys. Challenges children to mark a path from a table to the wastebasket with masking tape, then draw a map of the path, adding pictures of objects appearing along the path, such as a table or easel.

Content Area	Examples of Typical Knowledge and Skills From Age 3 ⟶ Age 6		Sample Teaching Strategies
Measurement	Recognizes and labels measurable attributes of objects (e.g., "I need a long string," "Is this heavy?"). Begins to compare and sort according to these attributes (e.g., *more/less, heavy/light*; "This block is too short to be the bridge").	Tries out various processes and units for measurement and begins to notice different results of one method or another (e.g., what happens when we *don't* use a standard unit). Makes use of nonstandard measuring tools or uses conventional tools such as a cup or ruler in nonstandard ways (e.g., "It's three rulers long").	Uses comparing words to model and discuss measuring (e.g. "This book feels heavier than that block," "I wonder if this block tower is taller than the desk?"). Uses and creates situations that draw children's attention to the problem of measuring something with two different units (e.g., making garden rows "four shoes" apart, first using a teacher's shoe and then a child's shoe).
Pattern/ algebraic thinking	Notices and copies simple repeating patterns, such as a wall of blocks with long, short, long, short, long, short, long....	Notices and discusses patterns in arithmetic (e.g., adding one to any number results in the next "counting number").	Encourages, models, and discusses patterns (e.g., "What's missing?" "Why do you think that is a pattern?" "I need a blue next"). Engages children in finding color and shape patterns in the environment, number patterns on calendars and charts (e.g., with the numerals 1–100), patterns in arithmetic (e.g., recognizing that when zero is added to a number, the sum is always that number).
Displaying and analyzing data	Sorts objects and counts and compares the groups formed. Helps to make simple graphs (e.g., a pictograph formed as each child places her own photo in the row indicating her preferred treat—pretzels or crackers).	Organizes and displays data through simple numerical representations such as bar graphs and counts the number in each group.	Invites children to sort and organize collected materials by color, size, shape, etc. Asks them to compare groups to find which group has the most. Uses "not" language to help children analyze their data (e.g., "All of these things are red, and these things are NOT red"). Works with children to make simple numerical summaries such as tables and bar graphs, comparing parts of the data.

References

Adams, M. 1990. *Beginning to read*. Cambridge, MA: MIT Press.

Baroody, A.J. 1987. *Children's mathematical development*. New York: Teachers College Press.

Baroody, A.J. 2004. The developmental bases for early childhood number and operations standards. In *Engaging young children in mathematics: Standards for early childhood mathematics education*, eds. D.H. Clements, J. Sarama, & A. DiBiase, 173–219. Mahwah, NJ: Lawrence Erlbaum.

Baroody, A.J., & J.M. Wilkins. 1999. The development of informal counting, number, and arithmetic skills and concepts. In *Mathematics in the early years*, ed. J.V. Copley, 48–65. Reston, VA: National Council of Teachers of Mathematics, and Washington, DC: NAEYC.

Basile, C.G. 1999. The outdoors as a context for mathematics in the early years. In *Mathematics in the early years*, ed. J. Copley, 156–161. Reston, VA: National Council of Teachers of Mathematics, and Washington, DC: NAEYC.

Beck, I.L., & M.G. McKeown. 2001. Text talk: Capturing the benefits of read-aloud experiences for young children. *The Reading Teacher* 55 (1): 10–20.

Beck, I.L., M.G. McKeown, & L. Kucan. 2002. *Bringing words to life*. New York: Guilford.

Bennett-Armistead, V.S., N.K. Duke, & A.M. Moses. 2005. *Literacy and the youngest learner: Best practices for educators of children from birth to five*. New York: Scholastic.

Benson, M.S. 1993. The structure of four- and five-year-olds' narratives in pretend play and storytelling. *First Language* 13 (38): 203–223.

Bowman, B.T., M.S. Donovan, & M.S. Burns, eds. 2001. *Eager to learn: Educating our preschoolers*. Washington, DC: National Academy Press.

Brown, A.L. 1989. Analogical learning and transfer: What develops? In *Similarity and analogical reasoning*, eds. S. Vosniadou & A. Ortony, 369–412. New York: Cambridge University Press.

Casbergue, R.M., & M.B. Plauche. 2003. Immersing children in nonfiction: Fostering emergent research and writing. In *Literacy and young children: Research-based practices*, eds. D.M. Barone & L.M. Morrow, 243–260. New York: Guilford.

Casey, B., J.E. Kersh, & M.J. Young. 2004. Storytelling sagas: An effective medium for teaching early childhood mathematics. *Early Childhood Research Quarterly* 19 (1): 167–172.

Caswell, L.J., & N.K. Duke. 1998. Non-narrative as a catalyst for literacy development. *Language Arts* 75 (2): 108–117.

Charlesworth, R., & K.K. Lind. 2003. *Math and science for young children*. 4th ed. Clifton Park, NY: Thomson Delmar.

Clements, D.H. 1999. Geometric and spatial thinking in young children. In *Mathematics in the early years*, ed. J.V. Copley, 66–79. Reston, VA: National Council of Teachers of Mathematics, and Washington, DC: NAEYC.

Clements, D.H. 2004. Geometric and spatial thinking in early childhood education. In *Engaging young children in mathematics: Standards for early childhood mathematics education*, eds. D.H. Clements, J. Sarama, & A. DiBiase, 267–297. Mahwah, NJ: Lawrence Erlbaum.

Cochran-Smith, M. 1984. *The making of a reader*. Norwood, NJ: Ablex.

Collins, M.F. 2004. *ESL preschoolers' English vocabulary acquisition and story comprehension from storybook reading*. Doctoral dissertation, Boston University.

Copley, J.V., ed. 1999. *Mathematics in the early years*. Reston, VA: National Council of Teachers of Mathematics, and Washington, DC: NAEYC.

Copley, J.V. 2000. *The young child and mathematics*. Washington, DC: NAEYC, and Reston, VA: National Council of Teachers of Mathematics.

Crain-Thoreson, C., & P.S. Dale. 1992. Do early talkers become early readers? Linguistic precocity, preschool language, and emergent literacy. *Developmental Psychology* 28 (3): 421–429.

Dickinson, D.K. 2001. Large group and free-play times: Conversational settings supporting language and literacy development. In *Beginning literacy with language*, eds. D.K. Dickinson & P.O. Tabors, 223–255. Baltimore: Paul H. Brookes.

Dickinson, D.K., A. McCabe, & N. Clark-Chiarelli. 2004. Preschool-based prevention of reading disabilities. In *Handbook of language and literacy: Development and disorders*, eds. C.A. Stone, E.R. Sulliman, B.J. Ehren, & K. Apel, 209–227. New York: Guilford.

Dickinson, D.K., A. McCabe, & M.J. Essex. 2006. A window of opportunity we must open to all: The case for preschool with high-quality support for language and literacy. In *Handbook of early literacy research, Vol. 2*, eds. D.K. Dickinson & S.B. Neuman, 11–28. New York: Guilford.

Dickinson, D.K., & M. Porche. 2005. *Long-term effects of preschool classroom interactions on the language and literacy skills of low-income children*. Paper presented at the biannual conference of the Society for Research in Child Development, 8 April, Atlanta, GA.

Dickinson, D.K., & M.W. Smith. 1994. Long-term effects of preschool teachers' book readings on low-income children's vocabulary and story comprehension. *Reading Research Quarterly* 29 (2): 104–112.

Duffy, G.G., & L.R. Roehler. 1989. Why strategy instruction is so difficult and what we need to do about it. In *Cognitive strategy research: From basic research to educational applications*, eds. C.B. McCormick, G. Miller, & M. Pressley, 133–154. New York: Springer Verlag.

Duffy, G.G., L.R. Roehler, E. Sivan, G. Rackliffe, C. Book, M. Meloth, et al. 1987. Effects of explaining the reasoning associated with using reading strategies. *Reading Research Quarterly* 22 (3): 347–368.

Duke, N.K., & J. Kays. 1998. "Can I say 'once upon a time'?" Kindergarten children developing knowledge of information book language. *Early Childhood Research Quarterly* 13 (2): 295–318.

Duke, N.K., D. Pearson, & S. Taberski. 2003. *Reading and writing informational text in the primary grades*. New York: Scholastic.

Duncan, G.J., C.J. Dowsett, A. Claessens, K. Magnuson, A.C. Huston, P. Klebanov, et al. 2007. School readiness and later achievement. *Developmental Psychology* 43 (6): 1428–1446.

Ehri, L.C., & J. Sweet. 1991. Fingerpoint-reading of memorized text: What enables beginners to process the print? *Reading Research Quarterly* 26 (4): 442–462.

Eimas, P.D., & P.C. Quinn. 1994. Studies on the formation of perceptually based basic-level categories in young infants. *Child Development* 65: 903–917.

Elley, W.B. 1989. Vocabulary acquisition from listening to stories. *Reading Research Quarterly* 24 (2): 174–187.

Epstein, A.S. 2007. *The intentional teacher: Choosing the best strategies for young children's learning*. Washington, DC: NAEYC.

Evans, C.W., A.J. Leija, & T.R. Falkner. 2001. *Math links: Teaching the NCTM 2000 standards through children's literature*. Englewood, CO: Teacher Ideas Press.

Ginsburg, H.P., N. Inoue, & K. Seo. 1999. Young children doing mathematics: Observations of everyday activities. In *Mathematics in the early years*, ed. J.V. Copley, 88–99. Reston, VA: National Council of Teachers of Mathematics, and Washington, DC: NAEYC.

Ginsburg, H.P., J.S. Lee, & J.S. Boyd. 2008. Mathematics education for young children: What it is and how to promote it. *Social Policy Report* 22 (1): 2–23.

Greenes, C., H.P. Ginsburg, & R. Balfanz. 2004. Big math for little kids. *Early Childhood Research Quarterly* 19 (1): 159–166.

Griffin, S. 2004. Number worlds: A research-based mathematics program for young children. In *Engaging young children in mathematics: Standards for early childhood mathematics education*, eds. D.H. Clements, J. Sarama, & A. DiBiase, 325–342. Mahwah, NJ: Lawrence Erlbaum.

Griffiths, R., & M. Clyne. 1991. *Books you can count on: Linking mathematics and literature*. Portsmouth, NH: Heinemann.

Hamre, B.K., & R.C. Pianta. 2001. Early teacher-child relationships and the trajectory of children's school outcomes through eighth-grade. *Child Development* 72 (2): 625–638.

Hart, B., & T.R. Risley. 1995. *Meaningful differences*. Baltimore: Paul H. Brookes.

Helm, J.H., & S. Beneke, eds. 2003. *The power of projects: Meeting contemporary challenges in early childhood classrooms—Strategies and solutions*. New York: Teachers College Press, and Washington, DC: NAEYC.

Helm, J.H., & L.G. Katz. 2001. *Young investigators: The project approach in the early years*. New York: Teachers College Press.

Heroman, C., & C. Jones. 2004. *Literacy: The creative curriculum approach*. Washington, DC: Teaching Strategies.

Hoff, E. 2006. Environmental supports for language acquisition. In *Handbook of early literacy research, Vol. 2.*, eds. D.K. Dickinson & S.B. Neuman, 163–172. New York: Guilford.

Hoff, E., & L. Naigles. 2002. How children use input to acquire a lexicon. *Child Development* 73 (2): 418–433.

Hong, H. 1999. Using storybooks to help young children make sense of mathematics. In *Mathematics in the early years*, ed. J.V. Copley, 162–168. Reston, VA: National Council of Teachers of Mathematics, and Washington, DC: NAEYC.

Huttenlocher, J., W. Haight, A. Bryk, M. Seltzer, & T. Lyons. 1991. Early vocabulary growth: Relation to language input and gender. *Developmental Psychology* 27 (2): 236–48.

Huttenlocher, J., M. Vasilyeva, E. Cymerman, & S.C. Levine. 2002. Language input and child syntax. *Cognitive Psychology* 45 (3): 337–374.

Jobe, R., & M. Dayton-Sakari. 2002. *Info-kids: How to use nonfiction to turn reluctant readers into enthusiastic learners*. Markham, Ontario: Pembroke.

Johnson, P. 2004. *Choice words: How our language affects children's learning*. Portland, ME: Stenhouse Publishers.

Juel, C. 1988. Learning to read and write: A longitudinal study of fifty-four children from first through fourth grade. *Journal of Educational Psychology* 80 (4): 437–447.

Justice, L.M., S. Chow, C. Capellini, K. Flanigan, & S. Colton. 2003. Emergent literacy intervention for vulnerable preschoolers: Relative effects of two approaches. *American Journal of Speech-Language Pathology* 12 (3): 320–332.

Kim, S.L. 1999. Teaching mathematics through musical activities. In *Mathematics in the early years*, ed. J.V. Copley, 146–150. Reston, VA: National Council of Teachers of Mathematics, and Washington, DC: NAEYC.

Klibanoff, R.S., S.C. Levine, J. Huttenlocher, & M. Vasilyeva. 2006. Preschool children's mathematical knowledge: The effect of teacher "math talk." *Developmental Psychology* 42 (1): 59–69.

Landry, S.H., K.E. Smith, & P.R. Swank. 2006. Responsive parenting: Establishing early foundations for social, communication, and independent problem-solving skills. *Developmental Psychology* 42 (4): 627–642.

Layzer, J.I., B.D. Goodson, & M. Moss. 1993. *Observational study of early childhood programs. Final report. Volume 1: Life in preschool.* Washington, DC: U.S. Department of Education.

Lonigan, C.J. 2006. Conceptualizing phonological processing skills in prereaders. In *Handbook of early literacy research, Vol. 2*, eds. D.K. Dickinson & S.B. Neuman, 77–89. New York: Guilford.

MacDonald, S. 2007. *Math in minutes: Easy activities for children ages 4–8.* Beltsville, MD: Gryphon House.

McCartney, K. 1984. Effect of quality of day care environment on children's language development. *Developmental Psychology* 20 (2): 244–260.

McClelland, M.M., F.J. Morrison, & D.L. Holmes. 2000. Children at risk for early academic problems: The role of learning-related social skills. *Early Childhood Research Quarterly* 15 (3): 307–329.

McGee, L.M., & J.A. Schickedanz. 2007. Repeated interactive read-alouds in preschool and kindergarten. *The Reading Teacher* 60 (8): 742–751.

Metsala, J.L., & A.C. Walley. 1998. Spoken vocabulary growth and the segmental restructuring of lexical representations: Precursors to phonemic awareness and early reading ability. In *Word recognition in beginning literacy*, eds. J.L. Metsala & L.C. Ehri, 89–120. Mahwah, NJ: Lawrence Erlbaum.

Morrow, L.B. 1987. The effects of one-to-one story readings on children's questions and comments. In *36th yearbook of the National Reading Conference*, eds. S. Baldwin & J. Readance. Rochester, NY: National Reading Conference.

Muter, V., C. Hulme, M.J. Snowling, & J. Stevenson. 2004. Phonemes, rimes, vocabulary, and grammatical skills as foundations for early reading development: Evidence from a longitudinal study. *Developmental Psychology* 40 (5): 665–681.

NAEYC & National Council for Teachers of Mathematics. 2002. *Early Childhood Mathematics: Promoting good beginnings.* A joint position statement of NAEYC and NCTM. Online: http://www.naeyc.org/about/positions/psmath.asp.

National Council of Teachers of Mathematics. 2000. *Principles and standards for school mathematics.* Reston, VA: Author.

Nelson, G.D. 1999. Within easy reach: Using a shelf-based curriculum to increase the range of mathematical concepts accessible to young children. In *Mathematics in the early years*, ed. J.V. Copley, 135–45. Reston, VA: National Council of Teachers of Mathematics, and Washington, DC: NAEYC.

Nelson, G.D. 2007. *Math at their own pace.* St. Paul, MN: Redleaf Press.

Neuman, S.B. 1990. Assessing inferencing strategies. In *Literacy theory and research*, eds. J. Zutell & S. McCormmick, 267–274. Chicago: National Reading Conference.

Neuman, S.B. 1999. Books Make a Difference: A Study of Access to Literacy. *Reading Research Quarterly* 34 (3): 286–311.

Neuman, S.B., C. Copple, & S. Bredekamp. 2000. *Learning to read and write: Developmentally appropriate practices for young children.* Washington, DC: NAEYC.

NICHD Early Child Care Research Network. 2005. Pathways to reading: The role of oral language in the transition to reading. *Developmental Psychology* 41 (2): 428–442.

Reutzel, D.R., P.C. Fawson, J.R. Young, T.G. Morrison, & F. Wilcox. 2003. Reading environmental print: What is the role of concept about print in discriminating young readers' responses? *Reading Psychology* 24 (2): 123–162.

Schickedanz, J.A. 1998. What is developmentally appropriate practice in early literacy?: Considering the alphabet. In *Children achieving: Best practices in early literacy*, eds. S.B. Neuman & K.A. Roskos, 20–37. Newark, DE: International Reading Association.

Schickedanz, J.A. 1999. *Much more than the ABCs: The early stages of reading and writing.* Washington, DC: NAEYC.

Schickedanz, J.A. 2003. Engaging preschoolers in code learning: Some thoughts about preschool teachers' concerns. In *Literacy and young children: Research-based practices*, eds. D.M. Barone & L.M. Morrow, 121–139. New York: Guilford.

Schickedanz, J.A. 2006. *Supporting story comprehension in preschool children: Use of comprehension asides.* Pre-conference institute of the annual meeting of the International Reading Association, 30 April, Chicago, IL.

Schickedanz, J.A. 2007. Increasing children's learning by getting to the bottom of their confusion. In *Achieving excellence in preschool literacy instruction*, eds. L.M. Justice & C. Vukelich, 182–197. New York: Guilford.

Schiro, M. 1997. *Integrating children's literature and mathematics in the classroom.* New York: Teachers College Press.

Schiro, M. 2004. *Oral storytelling and teaching mathematics: Pedagogical and multicultural perspectives.* Thousand Oaks, CA: Sage Publications.

Senechal, M., & J. LeFevre. 2002. Parental involvement in the development of children's reading skill: A 5-year longitudinal study. *Child Development* 73 (2): 445–460.

Senechal, M., G. Ouellette, & D. Rodney. 2006. The misunderstood giant: On the predictive role of early vocabulary to future reading. In *Handbook of early literacy research, Vol. 2*, eds. D.K. Dickinson & S.B. Neuman, 173–182. New York: Guilford.

Sipe, M. 1986. Good-morning poem. In *Read-aloud rhymes for the very young*, ed. J. Prelutsky, 48. New York: A. Knopf.

Smith, L.A. 2006. Think-aloud mysteries: Using structured, sentence-by-sentence text passages to teach comprehension strategies. *The Reading Teacher* 59 (8): 764–773.

Spira, E.G., S.S. Bracken, & J.F. Fischell. 2005. Predicting improvement after first grade reading difficulties: The effects of oral language, emergent literacy, and behavior skills. *Developmental Psychology* 41 (1): 225–234.

Stein, N.L. 1988. The development of children's storytelling skill. In *Child language: A reader*, eds. M.B. Franklin & S.S. Barten, 282–297. New York: Oxford University Press.

Storch, S.A., & G.J. Whitehurst. 2002. Oral language and code-related precursors to reading: Evidence from a longitudinal structural model. *Developmental Psychology* 38 (6): 934–947.

Teale, W.H., & M.C. Martinez. 1996. Reading aloud to young children: Teachers' reading styles and kindergarteners' text comprehension. In *Children's early text construction*, eds. C. Pontecorvo, M. Orsolini, B. Burge, & L.B. Resnick, 321–344. Mahwah, NJ: Lawrence Erlbaum.

Torgesen, J.K., A.W. Alexander, R.K. Wagner, C.A. Rashotte, K.K. Voeller, & T. Conway. 2001. Intensive remedial instruction for children with severe reading disabilities: Immediate and long-term outcomes from two instructional approaches. *Journal of Learning Disabilities* 34 (1): 33–58.

U.S. Department of Education, U.S. Department of Health and Human Services, Early Childhood-Head Start Task Force. 2002. *Teaching our youngest: A guide for preschool teachers and child-care and family providers*. Washington, DC: U.S. Department of Education.

Vasilyeva, M., J. Huttenlocher, & H. Waterfall. 2006. Effects of language intervention on syntactic skill levels in preschoolers. *Developmental Psychology* 42 (1): 164–174.

Vukelich, C., J.F. Christie, & B. Enz. 2008. *Helping young children learn language and literacy: Birth through kindergarten*. 2d ed. Boston: Pearson/Allyn and Bacon.

Weizman, Z.O., & C.E. Snow. 2001. Lexical input as related to children's vocabulary acquisition: Effects of sophisticated exposure and support for meaning. *Developmental Psychology* 37 (2): 265–279.

Williams, B., D. Cunningham, & J. Lubawy. 2005. *Preschool math*. Beltsville, MD: Gryphon House.

Children's Books

Arnosky, J. *Rabbits and raindrops.*

Arnosky, J. *Raccoon on his own.*

Beil, K.M. *A cake all for me.*

Carle, E. *Rooster's off to see the world.*

Collard, S.B. *Beaks!*

Crews, D. *Ten black dots.*

Ehlert, L. *Fish eyes: A book you can count on.*

Gray, S., & S. Walker. *Eye wonder: Birds.*

Hartley, K., C. Macro, & P. Taylor. *Caterpillar.*

Hennessy, B.G. *Jake baked the cake.*

Hutchins, H. *One dark night.*

Hutchins, P. *The doorbell rang.*

Kleven, E. *The puddle pail.*

Lionni, L. *A color of his own.*

Lionni, L. *Inch by inch.*

National Audubon Society. *Birds: First field guide.*

Prince, A.J., & G. Laroche. *What do wheels do all day?*

Root, P. *One duck stuck.*

Slobodkina, E. *Caps for sale: A tale of a peddler, some monkeys, and their monkey business.*

Stevens, J., & S.S. Crummel. *Cook-a-doodle-doo.*

Sturges, P. *The little red hen (makes pizza).*

Swinburne, S.R. *Unbeatable beaks.*

Waddell, M., & B. Firth. *Hi, Harry!*

Wadsworth, O.A., & A. Vojtech. *Over in the meadow: A counting rhyme.*

Early years are learning years

Become a member of NAEYC, and help make them count!

Just as you help young children learn and grow, the National Association for the Education of Young Children—your professional organization—supports you in the work you love. NAEYC is the world's largest early childhood education organization, with a national network of local, state, and regional Affiliates. We are more than 100,000 members working together to bring high-quality early learning opportunities to all children from birth through age eight.

Since 1926, NAEYC has provided educational services and resources for people working with children, including:

• *Young Children*, the award-winning journal (six issues a year) for early childhood educators

• **Books, posters, brochures, and videos** to support your work with young children and families

• **The NAEYC Annual Conference**, which brings tens of thousands of people together from across the country and around the world to share their expertise and ideas on the education of young children

• **Insurance plans** for members and programs

• **A voluntary accreditation system** to help programs reach national standards for high-quality early childhood education

• **Young Children International** to promote global communication and information exchanges

• **www.naeyc.org**—a dynamic Web site with up-to-date information on all of our services and resources

To join NAEYC

To find a complete list of membership benefits and options or to join NAEYC online, visit **www.naeyc.org/membership.** Or you can mail this form to us.

(Membership must be for an individual, not a center or school.)

Name_____

Address_____

City_____State_____ ZIP _____

E-mail _____

Phone (H)_____(W)_____

❐ New member   ❐ Renewal ID # _____

Affiliate name/number _____

To determine your dues, you must visit **www.naeyc.org/membership** or call 800-424-2460, ext. 2002.

Indicate your payment option

❐ VISA ❐ MasterCard ❐ AmEx ❐ Discover

Card #_____ Exp. date _____

Cardholder's name_____

Signature_____

Note: By joining NAEYC you also become a member of your state and local Affiliates.

Send this form and payment to

NAEYC,
PO Box 97156
Washington, DC 20090-7156